SEVEN·DAYS·IN·LONDON

by Carole and William Halden

DAY-BY-DAY ITINERARIES
Each with a theme

— DAY 1 —
Welcome to London
Changing of the Guard and the Original City Tour

— DAY 2 —
History and Tradition
poets and Beefeaters on parade

— DAY 3 —
A day in the City
whispers in St Paul's, money in the Bank

— DAY 4 —
Shopping in style
crowds in Harrods, pensioners in Chelsea

— DAY 5 —
Art and artists
Turner at the Tate, Manet at the Courtauld

— DAY 6 —
Seeing the famous
face to face at Tussaud's, close-up on movies

— DAY 7 —
Down the Thames
the old at Greenwich, the new at Docklands

STAYING AWHILE
cinemas and clubs, theatres and galleries
for those with time to spare

PEOPLE AND PLACES
_____ntary
seen each day

To help with the planning of future editions the authors would welcome
comments and reactions. Please write to:
Carole and William Halden, Honeysuckle Cottage, Mill Lane, Uplyme,
Lyme Regis, DT7 3TZ, England

CITY TRAVEL KIT

SEVEN · DAYS · IN
London

by

Carole and William Halden

Doubleday

New York   London   Toronto   Sydney   Auckland

introducing ...

... Seven Days in London, a new concept in guidebooks. From the first morning of waking in this exhilarating city, the book takes over. First, it presents a theme for each day whether the visit is one, two or seven days. Then it introduces, smoothly and without fuss, the treasures and splendours of the city. There is no need to struggle with complicated symbols, confusing opening times, tortuous explanations and endless history.

The text gives easy-to-understand directions, picks out in bold type sights really worth seeing - and explains why. The sequence of tours can begin on any day. Avoid the theme of *Shopping in style* on a Sunday and *Art and artists* on a Sunday morning: many museums open only after lunch then.

Finally, each part of every day is timed and the only interruptions are directions to the city's most delightful and welcoming restaurants for coffee, lunch, tea and dinner. At the end of the stay, this guide will have made sure that the very best of London has been seen, enjoyed and appreciated.

contributors

Ylva French who wrote the itineraries was for ten years in charge of public relations for the London Tourist Board. She is the author of *Blue Guide London*, several other guides and a quiz book on London.

David Loftus, creator of the collage on the cover, has shown at the Illustrators' Gallery and the Best of British Illustration Exhibition.

Michael Munday whose watercolour maps illustrate the itineraries is chairman of the Board of Governors of the Association of Illustrators.

Jennie Pearson, the illustrator for *People and Places*, was Resident Designer at Fremantle Art Centre, Perth, Western Australia.

Esmond Wright who wrote *People and Places* is a former Director of United States Studies and Professor of American History at the University of London. A member of the House of Commons, 1967-70, his most recent books are *Franklin of Philadelphia* and *Benjamin Franklin, his Life as he Wrote it*. He is the holder of the 1988 Franklin Medal of the Royal Society of Arts, presented by the Duke of Edinburgh.

the authors also wish to thank

Dr Adriano Agnati, Director, Dr Roberto Melis, Annamaria Mannucci and Fiorenza Frigoni, Touring Club Italiano

Sandie Dawe and staff at London Tourist Board

Capt David Horn, The Guards Museum

Ted Jones, Secretary, Burlington Arcade

Jill Moore, British Tourist Authority

Peter O'Riley, Bank of England Museum

and for pictures used in this book

Britain on View (BTA/ETB) except: page 8 The Guards Museum; pages 13, 18 & 19 London Tourist Board; pages 22, 23 & 25 Corporation of London; page 24 The Museum of London; pages 26 & 27 The Bank of England; page 32 General Trading Company; pages 33 & 46 Simon McBride; page 36 & 37 The National Gallery; pages 38 & 39 The Tate Gallery; page 40 permission of the Trustees of the Wallace Collection; page 41 Courtauld Institute Galleries; page 44 Madame Tussaud's; page 55 Design Museum; page 57 Royal Botanic Gardens Kew; page 59 The British Museum (Natural History); and page 61 London Transport Museum.

contents

A royal greeting

Across St James's Park to feed the ducks, Buckingham Palace to change the guard and, after a pub lunch, to Victoria for the Original Round London Sightseeing Tour

A visitor may feel that London, the most famous metropolis in the world, needs no introduction. Yet the capital is really a vast gathering of villages - from Kensington to Knightsbridge, Chelsea to Clapham. And if that is not confusing enough, there is a reluctance to display street nameplates.

As compensation, Londoners are generally patient and helpful. Ask directions and they will stop and listen carefully, give a clear reply and, before they can be thanked, walk on with a smile.

Today's tour is designed as a flexible and easy welcome. From *St James's Park* underground station follow *Park* signs and, outside, cross the road into **Queen Anne's Gate**. These elegant 18th century town houses - note the lamp stands and carved doorways, unique in London - are now used as offices. Straight ahead lies **St James's Park** and on the left is Wellington Barracks where the Guards will be lining up from about 11.00 before marching to Buckingham Palace to take over sentry duties.

For over 300 years the Guards have protected the Sovereign. The duty of standing guard outside Buckingham Palace rotates among the Foot Guards. The guard is changed each morning during the summer and every other day from mid-August to April (to check which day phone 730 3488).

Cross over **Birdcage Walk** named after an aviary established here by Charles II,   and enter

6

the park. Straight ahead is the lake. From the middle of the bridge there is a celebrated view of Buckingham Palace one way and Westminster the other.

This was the first royal park in London, created by Henry VIII in the 16th century. The artificial lake was added later and a variety of duck and waterfowl are bred here on Duck Island, protected by water from too much attention and feeding by visitors.

Royalty once strolled here, now it is more likely to be government ministers or civil servants who escape from their Whitehall offices for some fresh air. Crowds gather at **Buckingham Palace** for the Guard Change, so head for a position by the railings or on Queen Victoria's memorial opposite.

Alternatively, if it is not too crowded, cross the Mall to **St James's Palace**, where one part of the Guard Change starts. Follow these guards to Buckingham Palace for the main ceremony.

Or watch the parade form at the **Wellington Barracks** and then, as the guards leave to take up their positions inside the palace at 11.30, follow behind.

This is what happens: the Old Guard forms up in Friary Court, St James's Palace, at 11.00 with a Queen's or Regimental Colour and marches along the Mall. At the same time, the detachment of the Old Guard at Buckingham Palace is inspected while the New Guard gets ready at Wellington Barracks. The Old Guard detachment from St James's Palace enters Buckingham Palace forecourt through the south centre gate to join the others.

At 11.30 the New Guard, led by a regimental band, marches into the forecourt through the north centre gate. During the Changing of the Guard, music is played. The Captain of the Old Guard symbolically hands over the Palace keys to the Captain of the New Guard.

The Old Guard forms up and leaves through the centre gates at 12.05 to return to Wellington Barracks. The New Guard takes up 7

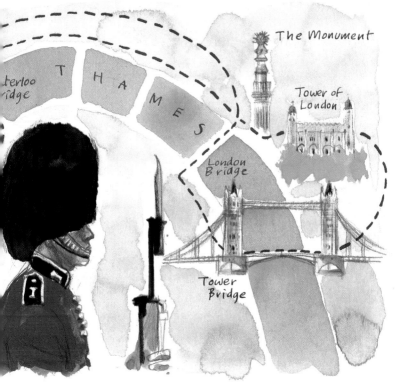

its post at Buckingham Palace. The St James's detachment leaves through the gates at 12.07 to take up its duties and march its Colour to the guardroom.

The Queen's Household Troops are responsible for protecting palaces at Windsor, the Tower of London and Horse Guards Parade and each has its own separate guard change. For Horse Guards, this takes place on the other side of St James's Park each day at 11.00.

The Guards Division comprises the Grenadier, Coldstream, Scots, Irish and Welsh Guards. All wear dark blue trousers, scarlet tunics and black bearskin caps.

They are identified by the colour of plumes in their bearskins. Grenadiers with a white plume on the left, the Coldstream by scarlet on the right, Irish by pale St Patrick's blue on the right and the Welsh by white and green on the left. Scots Guards do not wear plumes. Occasionally, when the Troops are serving abroad, the 8 honour of guard-mounting passes to another regiment - white-helmeted Royal Marines for instance, instead of the familiar bearskins.

After the ceremony, explore the **Guards Museum** at Wellington Barracks. Walk along Birdcage Walk past the parade ground to the gates leading to the **Guards Chapel**. The purpose-built under-ground museum is to the right. These are modern buildings; the chapel was destroyed in 1944 by a flying bomb and 121 died.

In the museum, the history of the five regiments of Foot Guards in peace and war is imaginatively illustrated. There are life-size model guards showing how uniforms differ. Also a painting of General Julius Caesar, of the Coldstream Guards, a colourful character who is reputed to have fought a duel in the 18th century with David Garrick over an actress, Peg Woffington.

The first section illustrates in date order the formation of the Grenadier, Coldstream and Scots Guards in the 17th century and the formation of the Irish and Welsh.

Battle honours on the Colours tell the story: the victories of the Duke of Marlborough and the triumphs of Wellington, the Iron Duke; gallantry in the Crimean campaign when the supreme award of the Victoria Cross was instituted and received by thirteen guards-men; bravery of the guards on the Somme and at Passchendale in the first world war and determination of the seventeen battalions in Europe and North Africa during the second; more recently, the exploits of the Scots Guards in the Battle of Mount Tumbledown in the Falklands.

Outside, turn left, past the Guards Museum shop, to the end of Birdcage Walk and left again into Buckingham Gate.

General Caesar: duellist

LUNCH: **This part of London, Victoria, is mainly an office area with lively pubs, winebars and restaurants. During the working week they tend to get busy in the lunch hour and tables at many places, even winebars, will be reserved. To maintain the atmosphere of tradition, try a delightful pub, The Colonies - first turn right along Buckingham Gate at No 25 Wilfred Street. In the summer this pub is a riot of colourful flowers with drinkers spilling out into the courtyard. The roast beef sandwiches are excellent. There is a fast**

Guard Change: playing in the New, out with the Old

turnround of people in a pub like this, so after a while there will be a chance to sit down.

Those who prefer something more substantial for lunch, or have children under 14 (not allowed in pubs), go to **Victoria Street** where, in Bressenden Place is Tavola Calda, a self-service Italian restaurant with a variety of hot and cold dishes.

After lunch, head for **Victoria Station**. Outside the entrance to the underground in Victoria Street is the starting point for the **Original Round London Sightseeing Tour** operated by London Transport. Look out for the bus stop with the bullseye symbol and the uniformed staff. These tours have qualified guides.

Double-decker buses, some of them open-topped, depart to match the demand and a top deck seat is worth a wait. The tour takes up to two hours. Reduced-price tickets are available if bought from London

Transport's ticket booth in Victoria Station. The bus heads first towards Belgravia to **Eaton Square**, home of London's wealthiest residents including the Duke of Westminster, then round **Belgrave Square**. Its attractive early 18th century houses are now embassies and worthy institutions.

On to **Hyde Park Corner**, busiest traffic hub in the capital, swinging past the former St George's hospital and then **Apsley House**, the first house inside the turnpike gate. This was the home of the first Duke of Wellington and is still lived in by his descendants. Its original address of No 1 London illustrates how the city has grown since the house was built in the late 18th century. A statue of Wellington on his horse Copenhagen is outside.

Inside is the **Wellington Museum** with beautifully furnished rooms, priceless paintings and Wellington memorabilia. Behind Apsley House is the gigantic statue of *Achille* paid for by 'women of England' and erected in honour of Wellington and his soldiers.

Up **Park Lane** with hotels and offices on the right and **Hyde Park** to the left - a spread of grass and trees as far as the eye can see. This is the largest park in London with its own lake, the Serpentine, in the centre. The bus turns right before **Marble Arch** and **Speakers' Corner** to **Grosvenor Square** with the massive **American Embassy** to the right, and continues into **Berkeley Square**, famous from the song *A Nightingale Sang in Berkeley Square.* Not many around today.

Next, the bus reaches **Regent Street** with its shops and stores. **Piccadilly Circus**, **Trafalgar Square** and **Whitehall** follow - look out for **Horse Guards Parade**, the **Cenotaph** and **Downing Street**.

Parliament Square may one day have its own fountain which would liven up this open space in front of the **Houses of Parliament**. Politicians can be seen interviewed here for television with the tower of **Big Ben** as a backdrop.

The bus heads for the other side of the **River Thames** along Millbank and across **Lambeth Bridge**. From this side there is a splendid view of the **Palace of Westminster** but don't forget to look right when the bus passes **St Mary's Church** which is now a Museum of Garden History. Both

10

Landmarks from the Original Round London bus tour: the Thames ...

the Tradescants (father and son), botanists and royal gardeners of the 17th century are buried here, as is Captain Bligh of the *Bounty*. The red-brick Tudor building is **Lambeth Palace**, home of the Archbishop of Canterbury, leader of the Church of England. On the left, the outline of the Houses of Parliament disappears behind **St Thomas' Hospital**. In the grounds is the new **Florence Nightingale Museum** with an evocative display on the single-minded campaign of this great woman to improve hospitals in war and peace.

The bus continues along past Westminster Bridge, **County Hall** - once the seat of London's local government - and then the **Royal Festival Hall** and other buildings of the **South Bank** arts complex before crossing **Waterloo Bridge** for another fine view of the river.

Into the **Aldwych** with BBC's overseas services on the right at **Bush House** and then on the left are the imposing **Royal Courts of Justice**. Look long and hard for any signs of 'Ink Street' in **Fleet Street** - once the home of the Press. All the national newspapers have moved - east to Docklands, west to Kensington High Street or south of the river. News agencies such as Reuters and the Press Association and provincial newspapers remain. At Ludgate Circus the bus turns south and then east along Queen Victoria Street passing the **Mermaid Theatre**. Over **London Bridge** then into Tooley Street, experiencing a renaissance with **Hays Galleria**, a shopping mall in a filled-in wharf with several visitor attractions including the **London Dungeon** and **Space Adventure**.

Across the river, on to **Tower Bridge** with the **Tower of London** to the left and **St Katharine's Dock** to the right. The bus now turns back along Upper Thames Street. On the left is **Billingsgate Market**, once London's wholesale fish market. It is now yet another commercial city building.

The **Monument** on the right at the top of Fish Street Hill was built to commemorate the Great Fire of London - spot the 'flames' on the top - its height of 62 metres matches the distance from the start of the fire in Pudding Lane in 1666.

Along the **Embankment**, past floating pubs and restaurants, including the old Thames barge

11

and the Embankment

Wilfred. On the right is **The Temple** with its **Inns of Court** - colleges of law and offices of lawyers - and further on, the façade of **Somerset House** housing the Courtauld Institute Galleries with its famous art collection. Next, the embankment gardens and ahead Big Ben and Parliament Square. On the left leaving the square is **Westminster Abbey**.

The bus returns along Victoria Street, with tall offices and, almost hidden, **Westminster Cathedral** on the left. Its square campanile 83 metres high is reached by lift and gives a splendid view of London.

TEA: A traditional English tea rounds off the afternoon. Cross Victoria Street, go left, over Buckingham Palace Road and next right into Beeston Place. Here is the last privately-owned grand hotel in London - The Goring. When it was built in 1910, by the grandfather of the present managing director, it was the first hotel in the world to be fitted with the luxuries of central heating and en-suite bathrooms. Tea is served in the lounge with a view of the small, unexpected garden. Finger sandwiches, scones and special Goring 'light fruit cake' offered from a trolley are accompanied by a range of teas including the hotel's special Ceylon blend.

Alternatively, turn right into

Buckingham Palace Road, past the front of the Palace - now much quieter - and bear to the left through Green Park. Ice houses were built to please Charles II and his court who picnicked here.

Cross Piccadilly and, to the left, is the Park Lane hotel where, in the elegant lounge, tea is served to the playing of a piano. If it is a weekend, go further afield to the Waldorf Hotel in the Aldwych (nearest tube is Embankment) and join the tea-dance in the Edwardian Palm Court.

After such a substantial tea, there is little need for an early dinner. Take the opportunity for a stroll to admire the floodlit memorials and buildings.

DINNER: **Londoners love fish and one of the best traditional seafood restaurants is Bentley's in Swallow Street. Walking from Piccadilly Circus, take the second right along Piccadilly. Oysters, smoked fish and crab are among the starters with scampi, salmon, sole, and scallops to follow and rich puddings and savouries. Meat eaters are not neglected in the range of fixed-price menus.**

Alternatively, just off Hyde Park Corner take the first turn left off Knightsbridge, Old Barrack Yard, and towards the end at 18 Wilton Row, is a traditional pub, the Grenadier. This was once the mess for the Duke of Wellington's officers, one of whom died after being flogged for cheating at cards. He haunts the pub in September. There is a sentry box outside and plenty of memorabilia inside, including one of the oldest pewter-topped bars. The à la carte dinner menu features Beef Wellington and the well-priced three-course table d'hôte includes Pork Genadier - fillet with orange sauce; and bread and butter pudding to follow. ❏

12

Introducing London

London covers 1,600 square kilometres. There is the West End with hotels, shops and theatres and the separately-administered City of London. The rest is divided into quarters - the East End and Docklands, South, West including Richmond and Hampton Court and North London.

The population of seven million grows by another 1.5 million who travel into central London to work. This means both the roads and public transport are busy 07.30 until 10.00 and 16.00 to 19.00. ❏

Boadicea and Big Ben march on

Standing on ceremony

**Churchill at the House, Shakespeare and Shelley in the Abbey,
lunch with Dickens and watching the Beefeaters
join Henry VIII on parade at the Tower**

History and tradition are still an intrinsic part of everyday life in London despite the encroachment of the 20th century. Today's tour explores London's historic places, all world-famous landmarks, where tradition comes to life every day.

Westminster Abbey is not just a place for coronations but also for royal funerals and weddings. In 1981, the Prince of Wales upset tradition by marrying in St Paul's Cathedral rather than Westminster Abbey. His choice was popular as the processional route was much longer, giving everyone a chance to see his bride Lady Diana and the magnificent carriages.

Arrive at *Westminster* underground station between 09.30 and 10.00. **Big Ben** opposite provides the perfect time-check. Actually, it is the name of the bell, not the clock. Famous all over the world from BBC broadcasts, the four dials and the Clock Tower have been re-gilded and sparkle magnificently in the sunshine.

The **Houses of Parliament** are being cleaned of a century's grime and soot - a worthwhile job since the Clean Air Act stopped the burning of coal in London in the 1960s and the pea-souper fogs famous from Sherlock Holmes stories have disappeared.

To the left is **Westminster Bridge**, the second bridge to be built over the river Thames and opened in the 18th century. A statue of Boadicea, the British queen who fought the Romans, adorns this side

14

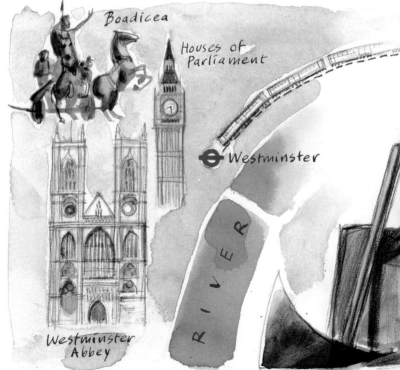

Boadicea

Houses of Parliament

Westminster

Westminster Abbey

RIVER

of the bridge. Cross the road and walk past the grand buildings of the Palace of Westminster - as the Houses of Parliament are also known. There was a royal palace on this site. **Parliament Square** is to the right with statues of famous men; notable is the striking figure of **Churchill** by Ivor Roberts-Jones looking straight at the House of Commons where he spent such a large part of his life.

A flashing light at the gate indicates that a taxi is requested by a Member of Parliament. At the far end of the palace is **Victoria Tower** - a flag flown here during the day and a light in the Clock Tower at night shows that the House is 'sitting' - in session.

One side of New Palace Yard, now planted with trees, is bordered by **Westminster Hall** - the most ancient part of the palace dated 1099. Pass the statue of Oliver Cromwell in front of it - another powerful man in British history. He overthrew Charles I and proclaimed a republic. Next on the left is the

St Stephen's Entrance to both Houses. The Commons Chamber was destroyed by a bomb during the war and reconstructed with gifts from Commonwealth countries. Beyond is the **House of Lords**.

Conducted tours of the Houses of Parliament require arrangements in advance with a Member, a Peer or an Embassy.

Watching the proceedings from the Strangers' Gallery of the House of Commons needs an application in advance to a Member. A few public seats are available by joining the queue at the St Stephen's Entrance; admittance is from 16.15 Mondays to Thursdays and 10.00 on Fridays.

The Houses of Parliament are in recess from the end of July to the end of October and for two weeks at Christmas, Easter and Whitsun.

Parliament's year opens in early November with a royal procession from Buckingham Palace, down the Mall, into Whitehall to Parliament Square. Crowds are relatively small for this occasion as it is a weekday.

The Queen and the royal family 15

16

enter through the House of Lords doorway and the Queen reads the Queen's Speech - the Government's programme for the year - from the throne in the House of Lords.

On the other side of the road is **Westminster Abbey.** Walk to the main entrance at the far end passing **St Margaret's Church**, original parish church of Westminster. Founded before 1189, this building dates from the late 15th century. It is the House of Commons church and frequently used for fashionable weddings. Samuel Pepys was married here in 1655, Milton for the second time in 1656 and Winston Churchill in 1908.

Enter the Abbey through the West Door and at the bookstall is an official detailed guide with a floor plan, useful for exploration.

The first substantial Norman abbey was consecrated on this site in 1065 during the reign of Edward the Confessor. Rebuilding was begun in the 13th century by Henry III and continued over the years; even Sir Christopher Wren was involved in changing the exterior. It is used for coronations, funerals and weddings of royalty, memorial services and other great occasions.

Walk along the left of the nave to the far end, passing the many different memorials - in the **North Transept** well-known politicians are commemorated.

Enter the North Ambulatory to explore one of the Abbey's most magnificent treasures - the **Chapel of Henry VII** in late-Perpendicular style or Tudor Gothic. Note the beautiful windows and carvings as well as the statues of saints. The chapel, commissioned by Henry VII, was completed in 1519. Here is the tomb of Elizabeth I which she shares with her sister Mary I.

In the **Royal Air Force Chapel** is the roll of honour of the 1,497 airmen who died in the Battle of Britain. Over the little bridge is the **Chapel of St Edward the Confessor** where the Shrine of St Edward erected in the 13th century is kept. Also in the shrine is the

Poets: The Brontës, Dylan Thomas Longfellow and Shakespeare

Coronation Chair (1300) and Stone of Scone, used for coronations. Originally the stone belonged to the Scottish kings and was brought here by Edward I. It was stolen by Scottish Nationalists in 1950 but recovered a few months later.

Poets' Corner is just ahead on the left in the South Transept. Many famous names can be found here: look for the bust of Henry Longfellow and that of William Blake by Epstein, graves of Robert Browning and Alfred Tennyson and memorials to T S Eliot and Lord Byron. Other writers include Wordsworth, Keats, Shakespeare and Shelley; also Kipling, Dickens and Thomas Hardy. Recent additions include Dylan Thomas, D H Lawrence and Edward Lear. Also in the Abbey are memorial plaques to Noel Coward and Lord Olivier.

Enter the **Cloisters** to see the Chapter House, the Pyx Chamber, Undercroft Museum and Treasury. The **Chapter House** dates from 1257 and was used by Benedictine monks as a meeting place. After the dissolution of the monasteries in 1540, the Exchequer used it to store government documents including the Domesday Book, the written record of a 1086 census of English landowners and property.

Pyx Chamber and **Treasury** were stores for valuables including sample coinage kept in wooden boxes or 'pyxes'. There is gold and silver plate from the Abbey and St Margaret's behind a massive door with six locks.

In the **Undercroft Museum** there are some remarkable funeral effigies of kings and queens and an ancient, stuffed parrot. In the cloisters is a Brass Rubbing Centre where, if time permits, souvenirs can be created.

Outside, is **The Sanctuary** with the new Queen Elizabeth II conference centre and Methodist Central Hall. Through the gate is Dean's Yard, used by boys from Westminster School.

Return to *Westminster* underground and take a train to *Tower Hill* station. At *Tower Hill*, turn left and follow the signs for **St Katharine's Dock**. From Tower Pier walk along the river past the Tower of London, under the bridge, to the dock.

St Katharine's Dock was once a thriving commercial dock. Only Ivory House remains of the original buildings. The dock is now a yacht haven. In addition to the Tower Hotel, there is a World Trade Centre and on the far side the new London Commodity Exchange.

LUNCH: Head for the Dickens Inn. Once a warehouse, now converted into a pub and restaurant and moved sixty metres to this spot. It was opened by the great grandson of Charles Dickens. On the ground floor is a pub serving sandwiches and salads. Of the restaurants, the Dickens Room serves fish and the Pickwick, traditional English food. It will take longer to eat here as the food is served à la carte but the surroundings are delightful.

Now it is time to explore the **Tower of London**. Past the Tower Hotel, under Tower Bridge, along the riverside wharf and through the west gate to the ticket offices on Tower Hill.

Tours of the Tower start from inside the gates led by a Yeoman Warder, more usually known as a Beefeater; allow up to an hour for this. Alternatively, explore the Tower with the help of the official guidebook on sale at the entrance.

On **Tower Green** is the site of

Yeoman Warder: on tour

17

The world's best-known jewel collection: the Crown Jewels

18

the scaffold where the famous lost their heads including two wives of Henry VIII. This is a good place to see the famous black ravens, which appear on most posters with the Beefeaters; according to legend the tower would fall if they flew away. Today their wings are carefully clipped - so the tower is likely to stand for yet a few more years.

The **Crown Jewels** in Waterloo Barracks are certainly worth seeing although it usually means a line which will move slowly but steadily downstairs past beautiful swords and sceptres, crowns and relics.

Do not miss the 12th century Anointing Spoon, oldest complete piece of the regalia; the Koh-i-nor diamond set in the Crown of Queen Elizabeth the Queen Mother; and the Maundy dish. Each year on Maundy Thursday, the Queen visits a different cathedral and dispenses specially-minted coins from this dish to worthy people. The number of coins coincides with her age.

The sceptre with the cross made for Charles II now holds the Star of Africa, 530 carats and the largest cut diamond in the world. The stone cut from the Cullinan Diamond, the Second Star of Africa, is set in the Imperial State Crown - which may not be there if the Queen is using it.

The fine **Royal Armouries**

collection is housed in the White Tower and Waterloo Barracks. On the third floor of the White Tower check the size of Henry VIII by his suit of armour, decorated by Hans Holbein in 1540; his horse had armour too. Among the Oriental armour in Waterloo Barracks is the striking Elephant armour brought back in the early 17th century by Lord Clive of India.

On the second floor of the White Tower is **St John's Chapel**, the oldest church in London dating from the 11th century - an example of pure Norman architecture. William the Conqueror built the White Tower and lived here with his family. His enemies ended up in the dungeons but the **Bloody Tower** has more gruesome associations. It has its own entrance from the Thames through **Traitors' Gate** and many who arrived here by boat under the portcullis never returned. The Little Princes, murdered here at the instigation of Richard III, gave the tower its name.

Every evening the Ceremony of the Keys takes place to ensure that the procedure for locking all the gates has been followed. Visitors who write in advance to the governor at the tower are allowed to watch. In the dark and without the thousands who throng the cobbled passageways, the terror of

prisoners incarcerated here can be imagined as sounds of heavy footsteps, clanking keys and slamming gates re-create this ceremony which has been carried out for 900 years.

On leaving the Tower turn left and return to St Katharine's Dock.

TEA: Into the Tower Hotel and, on the ground floor, the Which Way West cafe is the direction for tea or coffee. Or, for something stronger, on the first floor is the Thames Bar with a close-up view of Tower Bridge.

Tower Bridge looks as ancient as the Tower but it actually opened in 1894. Many people confuse this symbol of London with London Bridge further up, including, it is said, the American who bought the old London Bridge, now at Lake Havasu, Arizona.

Tower Bridge is the only bridge across the Thames which opens. Now that happens only a few times a week but when the Pool of London was busy with ships it was a regular occurrence. The walkways at the top allowed pedestrians to cross uninterrupted. Earlier this century these were a hang-out for pickpockets so they were closed.

The walkways were reopened in 1982. To reach them take the elevator to the top for a spectacular view up and down the river. Below are the drawbridges each weighing 1.25 million kilos and 52 metres in length. Cross the bridge by the walkway 43 metres above high water and on the other side is a museum illustrating the history of the bridge. On show are the original hydraulic steam pumping engines built in 1894 which, until electric power took over in 1977, raised the drawbridges half a million times.

19

DINNER: A day of history and tradition should end in the same way. At the Beefeater in the vaults of Ivory House at St Katharine's Dock enjoy a six-course banquet with wine and entertainment by Henry VIII and his courtiers. Lively and noisy with an opportunity to meet other visitors to London.

For those who prefer something quieter, but still traditional, there is Wiltons at the far end of Jermyn Street from Piccadilly Circus, No 55, the last genuine Edwardian restaurant left in London. The oysters are famous - either plain, in a cocktail or with a mornay sauce - and to follow are English-recipe pies, roasted game birds or mixed grills. Finish with a savoury, English cheese or crème caramel. ❏

Sounds of the City

Whispers in St Paul's, oratory of Rumpole at the Old Bailey, plague bell in the Barbican, clink of gold at the Bank and voices of Shakespeare

The square mile of the City of London is the most historic part of the capital. It is also an international commercial centre where millions of pounds, yen, dollars, francs and deutschmark change hands every day. Fragments of Roman London and the traditions surrounding the Lord Mayor contrast with the cut and thrust of the daily financial markets. And at weekends, with the City's streets deserted, buildings can be better admired and the history that interweaves with the concrete office blocks appreciated.

Travel by underground to *St Paul's* station and emerge through the *St Paul's* exit to street level.

Take in the view of **St Paul's** before exploring Wren's master-piece, allowing about one hour. The

first cathedral on this site was founded in the 7th century by Ethelbert. It was destroyed by fire as were four succeeding buildings - the current cathedral was saved only by the skill and hard work of volunteer fire-fighters when it was struck by wartime bombing in 1940.

The most spectacular sight must have been old St Paul's burning to the ground during the Great Fire of London. That was a very different building from the one standing here today. Londoners built their houses right up to the walls and used the huge cathedral for trading and gossip. Even horses passed through the church.

The work on the new cathedral started in 1675 and was completed in 1710. Go through the door on

20

St. Bartholomew the Great

Guildhall

The Old Bailey

St. Paul's

St. Paul's Cathedral

South Bridge

the left, past the statue of Queen Anne - St Paul's was completed during her reign. Follow the marked route through the cathedral to pass some of the great memorials, including the **Duke of Wellington's** to the left, listing on its base forty-eight of his battles.

Enter the choir: the gates in the sanctuary screen are by Jean Tijou. Then go through to the **American Chapel** (Jesus Chapel) with a roll of honour listing 28,000 Americans based in Britain who died in the war. The reconstructed chapel was opened by General Eisenhower in 1951. In the south choir aisle is the effigy of **John Donne**, a dean of St Paul's and a poet - the only statue to have survived the Great Fire.

Immediately left on leaving the sanctuary are stairs to the **Crypt** which extends below the cathedral. Here are the tombs of the Duke of Wellington and Admiral Nelson surrounded by memorials to other military and naval leaders. There is also the **Painters' Corner** with tributes to Landseer, Millais, Constable, Turner and others. Sir Christopher Wren's own tombstone is here and a model of his design for the cathedral.

The **Treasury** displays some of the vestments and embroideries belonging to St Paul's and other City churches. Take the stairs in the south transept to the galleries. The **Whispering Gallery** gives a good view of the paintings on the dome and whispers on one side against the wall are carried clearly to the other. The **Stone Gallery** on the outside of the building provides a panoramic view of London; sometimes the **Golden Gallery** above is open with an even better view but this will mean a total of 627 steps.

Outside, walk down Ludgate Hill on the right. A short way along is **St-Martin-within-Ludgate**, the least-altered Wren church in the city of London. Helped by the vestibule, the screen and extensive wood panelling it is a sanctuary of silence. Carved doorcases support an organ designed by Renatus Harris in the 17th 21

Lloyds of London

of nd

Royal Exchange ⊖ Bank

London Bridge

T H A M E S

century which features in lunchtime concerts. William Penn, father of the founder of Pennsylvania, was married here. On leaving, cross the road to appreciate the elegant needle spire of the church, a foil to the dome of St Paul's.

COFFEE: Take the next right into Old Bailey. On the left is Morris's, a busy sandwich bar with good coffee - but no beer.

Further along, on the right, is the **Old Bailey** Central Criminal Court made internationally famous by television's 'Rumpole of the Bailey'. The golden figure of *Justice* is at the top of the building with the Scales and Sword of Justice. The Old Bailey stands on the site of the notorious Newgate Prison where criminals were executed outside.

Straight ahead into Giltspur Street and, on the right, is **St Bartholomew's Hospital**, the oldest London hospital still standing on the same site. Right is West Smithfield with a small square of greenery in front of the huge central meat market.

Enter the hospital's quadrangle through the attractive gateway to see the stairway and hall of the 18th

Smithfield: cool joint

century buildings. The 12th century chapel, **St Bartholomew the Less**, was rebuilt in the 18th century and again in 1825 by Thomas Hardwick. Rahere, who founded the hospital after being saved from a serious illness in Rome, was a favourite courtier of Henry I, possibly even his jester. He also founded the Priory Church of **St Bartholomew the Great,** where he is buried.

Enter beneath its 13th century gateway, topped by an Elizabethan half-timbered building, to the right of the square. The brick tower of the church dates from 1628 and the five bells from 1510.

The church also survived the Great Fire but went through a period in the 18th century when it was used as workshops; even a blacksmith set up a forge inside. The Norman interior is attractive; the tomb of the founder Rahere is to the left of the altar with his wooden effigy beneath a canopy.

On Good Friday 'poor widows of the parish' receive hot cross buns placed on gravestones outside the church. As there are fewer 'poor widows' around today, it is mostly children who take advantage of this ancient ceremony.

Leave the church through the gateway and turn right into **Smithfield Market**, once 'smooth-fields' and the chief cattle and horse market for London since the 12th century. It was also a place of executions. The Bartholomew Fair held here every year was a jollier occasion with all of London taking part in festivities which lasted several days. But this became too exuberant and was stopped in 1840.

The present meat-market (no live cattle) is the only wholesale market still remaining in central London. It is a hive of activity from late at night when refrigerated lorries start arriving. Walk through the **Grand Avenue** in the middle of the market and between giant carcases hanging from hooks.

LUNCH: Into Charterhouse Street, turn right and at No 115 is the famous Fox and Anchor pub, serving the best breakfast

22

23

The City of London: dome of St Paul's, offices of the bankers

in London. **Pubs around the market can serve alcohol from early in the morning, but only to market workers. Excellent rump-steaks enjoyed by the meat porters are also served at lunchtime. Squeeze into the long bar and ask for a table. If a huge meal seems daunting, there are sandwiches at the bar. And if too crowded postpone lunch for the moment.**

In the nearby **Charterhouse Square** is a monastery founded in the 14th century. On the left is the 15th century gatehouse to Sutton's **Hospital in Charterhouse**. The buildings were bombed in 1941 but still house 'forty poor brethren', male pensioners who are members of the Church of England and of a suitable background.

Walk through to Aldersgate Street, turn right and left at the junction, through the Beech Street entrance to the **Barbican Centre**, considered to be the largest arts, conference and exhibition centre in

Western Europe. During the war this area was virtually demolished by bombing. It was redeveloped during the 1960s and 1970s and the Barbican Centre was opened by the Queen in 1982.

There is an art gallery on level 8, exhibitions and performances in the foyer and free concerts at lunchtime. The London Symphony Orchestra is based here at the concert hall which also hosts visiting international orchestras and soloists. The magnificent theatre, seating 1,100, is the London home of The Royal Shakespeare Company.

LUNCH: For those who waited, there is Waterside, the self-service cafe overlooking the lake, or the restaurant on level 7, The Cut Above, which also serves brunches at weekends.

Leave this part of the Barbican Centre by the Lakeside exit, walk along Aldersgate Street and follow the signs for **Museum of London**. This is one of London's best conceived museums. Start near the shop - the official booklet is useful.

Follow the direction signs and London's history unfolds stage by stage. There is a glimpse of a real Roman wall, through a large glass window. The name Barbican is explained - it meant fortress and was just one of many watchtowers on the wall that surrounded the City of London.

Exhibits include the Roman leather bikini trunks (possibly worn by an acrobat), the plague bell rung to warn passers-by that the victims of the dreaded disease were to be picked up and the re-enactment of the Great Fire of London which is repeated every eight minutes. Downstairs, in the **Late Stuart** section, is an inlaid backgammon board presented to Samuel Pepys by James II.

The prison cell and entrance door in the **Georgian London** section evoke conditions in prisons such as Newgate. **19th Century London** includes a model of the Crystal Palace of 1851 and the Euston Arch, both now destroyed. The shops, offices and pubs of this period are worth exploring, before moving to **20th Century London** and, finally, the Lord Mayor's coach which dates from 1757 and is still used once a year as the centrepiece for the Lord Mayor's procession.

TEA: Stop for tea or coffee in the museum's cafe as there will be few places for refreshments later in the heart of the City.

Leave the museum and turn left to pass the **Wesley Conversion Memorial** in the shape of a gigantic page from his journal. A walkway leads across the busy London Wall. Down the stairs into Noble Street and immediately on the right are the remains of a Roman Fort. Further down Noble Street on the right is the red-brick church of St Anne and St Agnes built by Wren in 1680 but almost destroyed in the war and reopened in 1966. Turn left into Gresham Street, continue until King Street and turn left into the **Guildhall**. This is the Hall of the Corporation of the City of London and dates from the 15th century.

To the right of the Guildhall, an extension is being built to house the City of London art collection but, rather inconveniently, the remains of a Roman amphitheatre, the first discovered in London, was found as work started.

Enter through the glass doors and ask for the **Great Hall** where the Court of Common Council which runs the City of London meets every third Thursday. The very impressive hall looks splendid, especially when set up for a state

24

Lord Mayor's coach: allowed out once a year

The Guildhall crypt: medieval artistry below the Great Hall

banquet. On the left is a statue of *Churchill* by Oscar Nemon, several other interesting sculptures and the wooden figures of *Gog* and *Magog*, the mythical founders of pre-Roman London, in the gallery. To see the medieval crypt ask at the desk.

Leave the Guildhall, turn left along Gresham Street and right into Prince's Street with the walls of the Bank of England to the left. Continue to the end of the street.

Six routes meet at this ancient crossroads, **the Bank**. Opposite is the **Mansion House**, home of the Lord Mayor of London. Cross to the left in front of the imposing **Royal Exchange**. The Jubilee Walkway Indicator identifies the important buildings. The Royal Exchange has its own 55-metre campanile topped by a golden weather vane carrying a grass-hopper - the crest of Gresham who founded the first Royal Exchange in 1564.

The Exchange was then a market and shops still remain at the side of the building. Since 1720 it has been headquarters for Royal Exchange Assurance, now Guardian Royal Exchange. Another tenant in the building, now with an addition of two. storeys, is the **London International Financial Futures Exchange** which operates in a shell so that the murals and the Turkish floor paving are not damaged. In front of the Exchange is a statue of

25

Writings on the wall

Blue ceramic plaques on houses and buildings throughout London are a familiar sight. They go back over a century to the Royal Society of Arts 'tablets' erected on buildings where famous people had lived. There are now some 600 blue plaques, from Jane Austen to van Gogh, Charlie Chaplin to Voltaire. Sometimes it is not the original building to which the plaque is fixed but its replacement. Proposals for new plaques are put forward all the time but the rules specify that the person should have made a contribution to human welfare or happiness and he or she must have been dead for twenty years or past the centenary of his or her birth. ❏

the Duke of Wellington on his horse and on the piazza's street lamps are the coats of arms of the leading city livery companies.

Across the road is the 'Old Lady of Threadneedle Street' - the **Bank of England**. The absence of windows on the lower ground floors is a security feature introduced after the Gordon Riots of 1780 when a mob marched on the bank. The bank also had its own military guard for nearly 200 years. To the side of the bank is the **Museum of the Bank of England**. Cross the road and turn right along Threadneedle Street and left into Bartholomew Lane. The gatekeeper wears a tailcoat in 'Houblon pink', named after the first governor of the bank, except for governors' meetings when he wears ceremonial robes.

The first room re-creates the original bank stock office with wax models in 18th century dress. At the information desk there is a free museum guide.

Exhibits include the historic Charter of 1694 - the starting capital had been raised in eleven days. Early notes featured the medallion of Britannia as security and this has since appeared on all banknotes. There is a large display of these.

In the centre of the rotunda is a pile of gold bars - all facsimile. However, the beautiful collection of silver is genuine. The interactive visual displays include financial questions and answers and up-to-date price information on gilts and shares. Chocolate gold bullion and other souvenirs, all made in Britain, can be bought.

Outside and on Threadneedle Street, walk further along to the **International Stock Exchange**, transformed since the 1986 'Big Bang' when dealing by computer was introduced.

Cross the road from the Stock Exchange building and walk down the alley behind Royal Exchange past the statue of Baron Reuters who founded the news agency.

Turn left into Cornhill and head for Lloyd's of London. On the way is St Michael's Alley with the tall tower of **St Michael**. On the right at the corner with Gracechurch

26

Gatekeeper: top hat and robes ...

Street is the church **St Peter's**, one of the many Wren churches in the City built between 1677 and 1681.

Leadenhall Market is across Gracechurch Street. The 100-year old building has been restored and includes traders selling traditional meat and game, as well as croissant and coffee shops.

Along Leadenhall Street and at the corner of St Mary Axe stands **St Andrew Undershaft** built in

and safe as the Bank of England

which also houses an exhibition on the history of insurance. The firms of underwriters use open offices or 'boxes' designed to look like the benches in Edward Lloyd's coffee-house where insurance started in 1688. The Lutine Bell, recovered from *HMS Lutine* in 1799, in the middle of the ground floor, used to be struck every time there was a disaster at sea; now it is used only for ceremonial occasions.

Walk round the building to examine the unusual design which concentrates all the services in vast tubes on the exterior, including two outside lifts.

Leave Lloyd's and return to *Bank* underground station.

For the evening, return to the City and the **Royal Shakespeare Theatre** in the Barbican or book for the **National Theatre** on the South Bank. These venues are the two major subsidized theatre companies in London with three theatres at one and two at the other.

DINNER: At both of these theatres it is possible to enjoy a sandwich or meal in the bars and restaurants. Those who prefer to eat after the theatre will find it relatively easy to reach Covent Garden from both the National and the Barbican. Two restaurants almost side by side are Joe Allen at 13 Exeter Street (836 0651) with American-style food and an informal atmosphere which attracts actors after the show; and Orso, 27 Wellington Street (240 5269), Italian nouvelle cuisine. Neither accept credit cards. Booking is essential for both - check with the theatre when the play ends and add half an hour from the National Theatre and forty-five minutes to one hour from the Barbican.

Chinatown in Soho is good for late-night eating with dozens of Chinese restaurants; booking is not needed, except for large parties, although there may be a short queue at the popular places. Try Mr Kong or Fung Shing both in Lisle Street near Leicester Square. ❏

1532, with its famous monument to John Stow who recorded events in the City in the 16th century. His quill pen is ceremoniously renewed each year by the Lord Mayor.

On the right in Lime Street is the striking new glass and steel building of **Lloyd's of London** by architect Richard Rogers. Visitors can see the Underwriting Room, with the Lutine Bell, from the visitors' gallery on the fourth floor

27

By appointment to ...

**Trading with the Court of St James, joining the world at Harrods,
keeping up with Princess Diana and the 'Sloanes'
and stepping out with the pensioners of Chelsea**

A London shopping experience is just as unique to the capital as Westminster Abbey or the Tower of London and even determined non-shoppers will enjoy visiting London's historic shops and arcades and exploring Harrods.

From *Piccadilly* underground station take the *Piccadilly/Lower Regent Street* exit. Walk down Lower Regent Street and take first right into **Jermyn Street**. Here are 18th century shops established to serve the Ladies and Gentlemen of the Court of St James's and which still serve royalty, ladies and gentlemen - now from all parts of the world.

Immediately on the right is **Geo F Trumper**, the Gentleman's Hairdresser and Perfumer, first

28

established in 1875. In the window is a display of shaving brushes and the fragrances traditionally used by royalty who still favour the establishment with their warrant.

Bates the Hatter follows - this is the place to buy an English bowler hat, symbol of the British 'Establishment' or a deer-stalker à la Sherlock Holmes. A shirtmaker next; order a made-to-measure shirt here or from one of the better-known shirtmakers in the street, Hilditch & Key or Turnbull & Asser at No 70. Downstairs at Turnbull's, devoted to their distinctive shirts, is called the Churchill Room after one of their famous customers. A wartime green velvet siren suit made for him is on display.

On the left is **St James's**

Church - a Wren church originally designed to face Jermyn Street. The friendly Wren Coffee Shop serves coffee and tea and wholesome food. At weekends in the open space at the front of the church - towards Piccadilly - there is a street market.

On the left-hand side is one of Jermyn Street's most famous shops: **Paxton & Whitfield** the cheesemonger established by a Suffolk cheesemaker in 1740. Go inside to admire the display of 300 European cheeses of which fifty are British farmhouse productions. Do not hesitate to ask for a sliver to taste.

Almost next door is **Floris** the perfumers which holds both the Queen's and the Prince of Wales' royal warrants. Juan Floris came from Minorca with his fragrances in the 18th century for ladies, courtesans, and gentlemen of the Court. The business is now run by the eighth generation of the family.

Two doors further on, to the right of the entrance to **Hilditch & Key,** is a blue plaque marking where scientist Sir Isaac Newton lived. Across the road is the refurbished **Princes Arcade** with its black and white marble floor.

COFFEE: Further along on the corner is the entrance to Fortnum and Mason's Fountain Restaurant. Enjoy a coffee and croissant at the table or the bar and afterwards go through to admire the tea and speciality counters of this elegant and renowned food store.

If it is near the hour go out through the main doors of the store and cross Piccadilly - carefully, looking right for buses and left for traffic. Watch as the figures of **Mr Fortnum and Mr Mason** emerge from the clock on the façade and bow to each other.

A few doors from Fortnum's are the twin bow-fronted windows of **Hatchards**, established in 1797 and the oldest bookseller in London. It is the proud holder of all four royal warrants - from the Queen, the 29

Duke of Edinburgh, the Queen Mother and the Prince of Wales.

Return to Jermyn Street down the side of Fortnum's to admire its green-trimmed windows. Turn right at the lights and another shop catering for gentlemen - **Alfred Dunhill**. Enter **Piccadilly Arcade** on the right, passing the **Armoury of St James's** selling toy soldiers and **Gered** with a selection of Wedgwood porcelain and Waterford crystal. Cross Piccadilly to explore the **Burlington Arcade** opposite. This is the longest of London's shopping arcades and dates back to the early 19th century.

Lord Cavendish built it for 'the gratification of the public and to give employment to industrious females'. His ideal was achieved later in the 19th century - but in an unexpected way. The arcade was notorious for high-class prostitution and a magazine warned that it was 'no place for a vicar'. It is guarded by 'Beadles' in their gold-braided top-hats and frock-coats who ensure that there is no running, no singing or other unseemly behaviour. They are Britain's oldest and smallest private police force.

Back on to Piccadilly, bear right and cross to St James's Street. Walk down on the left-hand side

Burlington Arcade: no running

passing **White's Club** (in a white late-18th century building with a bow-window - no name on the door), the oldest and grandest of the gentlemen's clubs of St James's. These were then popular as meeting places for gentlemen and several later became gambling clubs - now only permitted in licensed casinos.

Further down also on the left is **Boodles Club** with an attractive Georgian façade featuring a large window.

Almost opposite is **Brooks's Club**. Also across the road is the **Carlton Club**, Conservative party stronghold - it had to make an exception to its men-only rule to admit Margaret Thatcher as the only Lady Honorary Member.

Continue down past the modern headquarters of the *Economist* magazine stopping at **Lock & Co**, hat-makers since 1676 with a royal warrant from the Duke of Edinburgh. Past customers have included Beau Brummel, the Duke of Wellington and Lord Nelson.

Further down at No 3 behind the Georgian shop-front with the original 'Sign of the Coffee Mill' over the door is wine merchant **Berry Bros and Rudd**. The Texas Legation was here from 1842 to 1845, marked by a plaque in the passage-way leading to Pickering Place, London's smallest square.

The picturesque brick building at the end is **St James's Palace** with a lone sentry. This is where the royal family lived during the 18th century until Queen Victoria moved to Buckingham Palace. The gatehouse with its four octagonal towers is 16th century. The palace is used as offices by the royal family and the staterooms for functions. Here, foreign ambassadors are accredited to the Court of St James's although they and their credentials are later presented to the Queen at Buckingham Palace.

Walk up the other side of St James's Street. See the **Royal Overseas League** in Park Place, then turn left into Benet Street. On the corner with Arlington Street is the Blue Posts pub. Continue right past the side entrance of **the Ritz** with its famous Palm Court setting

30

Harrods: treasured tiles above the food halls

for teas. Turn left on to Piccadilly to *Green Park* underground station. Take the Piccadilly line two stops to *Knightsbridge*.

At *Knightsbridge*, leave by the sign *Sloane Street*. This junction and the roads leading from it form a heartland for sophisticated shops. Cross into **Harvey Nichols**, a beautifully laid-out fashion store for men and women. In the basement is the store's boutique Zone, the ground and the next three floors are devoted to designer fashion, the fourth to home furnishings and the top floor to toys and gifts.

Outside, return past the station and along Brompton Road.

Harrods, established in the mid-19th century by a tea-merchant, is the world's most celebrated store. It has more than 300 departments on five floors and can provide anything from tourist information on the fourth floor to a pedicure or a pet. Everyone makes their own way round - in great confusion initially. These are the highlights: the **Food Halls** are famous and justly so. Admire the bakery and charcuterie, the fruit and flowers and most especially the meat and fish hall. Do not forget to look up at the tiled ceilings, now officially protected. In the meat hall, they aptly portray *The*

Hunt with cheerful maidens and animals pursued by hunters, made by Royal Doulton in 1902.

Chocolates and confectionery 31 are attractive, particularly in their Harrods wrappings. There is also a healthfood bar away from the crush.

Celebrities sign their books at frequent lunchtime sessions in the vast 2nd floor book department. Kirk Douglas, Anthony Burgess, Joan Collins and Anita Brookner have recently added dedications to customers' copies. A selection of signed books is always available.

LUNCH: The fourth floor Georgian Restaurant is a self-service carvery, ample delicious looking roast meats. Next to it is the quiet Terrace Bar - open roof in summer - serving sandwiches and drinks. There are other restaurants including the self-service Upper Circle.

Outside, go left and a short way along, left again into Beauchamp Place, a chic narrow street with boutiques and restaurants. At the end go straight into Pont Street, with its gabled buildings and terra cotta decorations described as 'Pont Street Dutch'. On the corner is the Cadogan Hotel where Oscar Wilde was arrested. Turn right along Sloane Street and continue as far as the **General Trading Company** on the right. Explore this gifts and furnishings emporium popular with the Princess of Wales. She and other head-scarfed, well-off young ladies acquired the name 'Sloane Rangers' from this area. Its toy department has a colony of bears that includes the fashionable Sloane Rangers Henry and Caroline.

TEA: In the terrace basement of General Trading Company is the delightful cafe run by fashionable foodie Justin de Blank. Freshly-made pastries, scones with dollops of cream or sinful pot au chocolat.

Continue on to Sloane Square. The statue in the middle is Sir Hans Sloane, a physician who lived nearby and gave his name to the square. His collection of 80,000 items, from mineral specimens to manuscripts, began the British Museum.

32 Go across the square to the **Peter Jones** store for any useful shopping - from here **King's Road**

is mostly fashion and antiques. It was famous in the 'swinging sixties' when Mary Quant started her first shop, Bazaar, at No 138.

Usually on Saturday afternoons, at Royal Avenue on the left, 'punks' assemble. Punk fashion started in the King's Road where the Sex Pistols pop-group found a shop which sold leather, chains and other gear.

Look down Royal Avenue - the **Royal Hospital Chelsea** for army pensioners lies beyond. The In-Pensioners are often seen in this area in their striking scarlet coats with one of two hats - a black tricorne or a navy shako.

Further down the King's Road, still on the left, is Chelsea Old Town Hall. Continuing on, take the fourth left into Old Church Street and walk towards the river. The 12th century **Chelsea Old Church** has a chapel dedicated to Sir Thomas More whose statue is outside.

Turn left along **Cheyne Walk** then left into Cheyne Row and at No 24 is **Carlyle's House**. In this small unpretentious house still without electricity lived Thomas Carlyle,

General Trading Company: sin in the basement

Cheyne Walk: blue plaques where the famous lived

one of the 19th century's most influential British writers and thinkers. Back in Cheyne Walk, check for blue plaques showing the houses once occupied by famous people. Go across the junction and along Royal Hospital Road, past the National Army Museum and the Royal Hospital. Lower Sloane Street leads back to Sloane Square and the *Sloane Square* underground.

DINNER: After a day's shopping relax over a meal in an elegant restaurant. For a contrast in styles, choose between: Bombay Brasserie (370 4040), Bailey's Hotel, Gloucester Road, a large, airy restaurant with palms and ceiling fans and superb Indian regional cooking; or Columbus (589 8287) at 8 Egerton Gardens Mews (parallel to Brompton Road, off Egerton Terrace) stylish with a French brasserie atmosphere and zingy fresh food à la California. This new restaurant is run by food critic and television personality Loyd Grossman and his brother Neal. Good value - even wines are price-banded.   ❏

A touch of the British

**Appreciating Constable's *Hay Wain* and Gainsborough's
Morning Walk, smiling at Hogarth's satirical *Roast Beef*
then tea at The Savoy and pies at Porters**

London's galleries are famous and numerous. Today's tour covers four that are very different, selecting only the most interesting exhibits at each.

Though the **National Gallery** was started late by comparison with those of other European cities, it is one of the most comprehensive western art collections in the world. The paintings were first shown in this purpose-built building in 1838. The gallery has been extended several times and there is still not enough space to show all the works. In 1988 building started on the new wing to the left of the gallery looking from Trafalgar Square. This was paid for by the Sainsbury Trust.

The first design was rejected after the Prince of Wales referred to it as 'a carbuncle on the face of Trafalgar Square'. Robert Venturi's design which earned royal approval is in style with the old building.

Be sure to arrive at the gallery as the doors open at 10.00, except on Sundays when, like all major galleries, opening time is 14.00. It is an easy walk from *Charing Cross* underground. Go through to the bookshop and pick up the *Quick Visit to the National Gallery* leaflet which reproduces and locates sixteen of the 2,000 major works.

Return to the foyer. Set into the floor of the vestibules are mosaics by Boris Anrep featuring celebrities such as Bertrand Russell, Greta Garbo, Winston Churchill and Margot Fonteyn. Turn right to **Room 1** for the

34

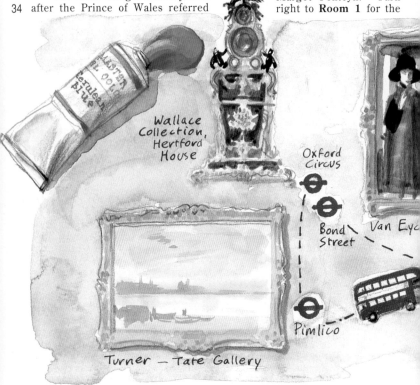

Wallace Collection, Hertford House

Oxford Circus

Bond Street

Van Eyc

Pimlico

Turner — Tate Gallery

Wilton Diptych from the late 14th century, one of the oldest paintings in the gallery, painted on both sides and hinged to shut like a book.

Further on in **Room 7** is the **Leonardo da Vinci** cartoon *The Virgin and Child with Saint Anne and St John the Baptist* - a delightful drawing full of joy and sweetness.

The story of *Bacchus and Ariadne* is the subject of the **Titian** in **Room 13** which was cleaned in 1969 to show the original, glorious colours. In **Room 24 Jan van Eyck's** symbolic portrait of the swearing of vows in *The Arnolfini Marriage* needs little introduction; **Rembrandt's** *Self Portrait aged 63* in **Room 27** is sad - he died the year it was painted. Nearby is his more cheerful *A Woman Bathing in a Stream* - she was his mistress.

One of the best **Turners** *The Fighting Téméraire* is in the British School section **Rooms 35-36** and **38-39**; also shown is **Constable's** rural *Hay Wain*, **Gainsborough's** elegant portrait of *Mrs Siddons*, the romantic picture *The Morning Walk*

and **Hogarth's** satirical series *Marriage à la Mode*. Finish with **Seurat's** *The Bathers* in **Room 45**.

COFFEE: There should be time now for coffee in the cafe in the basement - nice pastries and sandwiches too.

Upstairs, leave by the main entrance and go clockwise round the square to **Whitehall**. Look for the No 88 bus stop on the left. On the bus ask for the Tate Gallery.

This bus follows an interesting route, first passing **Horse Guards Parade**, then **Banqueting House** on the left with its beautiful painted ceiling, government offices on both sides, the **Cenotaph** in the middle of the road and **Downing Street** on the right. It then goes into **Parliament Square**, past the **Houses of Parliament**, along Millbank. Across the road from the bus stop is the Tate.

The **Tate Gallery**, opened in 1897, was funded by sugar magnate Henry Tate - hence the name. Here 35

-National Gallery

Charing Cross

Cezanne - Courtauld Institute, Somerset House

Waterloo Bridge

THAMES

is the national collection of British paintings from the 16th century to around 1900 as well as modern British and foreign paintings.

This visit concentrates on the **Turner Collection** in the Tate's **Clore Gallery**. Turn right at the steps leading to the main entrance. Cross the garden for the new wing.

The three-storey building with Japanese overtones was designed by James Stirling and was opened in 1987 by the Queen. J M W Turner bequeathed these 300 oil paintings and 20,000 sketches to the nation when he died in 1851. Pick up the free guide at the desk.

The second floor galleries include Turner's most famous paintings as well as some not seen widely before. **Gallery 107** illustrates his early work in oil including landscapes, marine paintings such as the famous *Shipwreck*; also biblical and historical works, including *Snow Storm: Hannibal and his Army crossing the Alps*.

Gallery 108 explores England and working life, some in the Dutch tradition, a result of his visit to the Low Countries in 1817; note *Frosty Morning* and *Entrance of the Meuse* and the very grand *England: Richmond Hill on the Prince Regent's Birthday*. Turner lived at Richmond for many years. In the **Gallery 103** some of his sketches

and studies are on view. Classical mythology based on the several journeys he made to Italy, is explored in **Gallery 106** in such paintings as the golden *Decline of the Carthaginian Empire*.

The Devon countryside is the inspiration for *Crossing the Brook* - his daughters are the models. More Italian inspiration in **Gallery 104**, showing the influence of the French painter Claude. The room is dominated by *Rome from the Vatican* which was a central picture in Turner's development.

In **Gallery 102** Turner moves on to explore colour and light in paintings from Petworth, Sussex, and the Isle of Wight, for example *Chichester Canal* and *Music at East Cowes Castle*.

Turner visited Venice and these paintings are shown in **Gallery 105**. The late works in **Gallery 101** are varied and include the lyrical and translucent *Norham Castle*. In **Gallery 109**, some of Turner's watercolours are on view.

If there is time before lunch to see more of the Tate, here are some of the many highlights:

Gallery 2 includes *Calais Gate (O the Roast Beef of Old England)* one of the best paintings of **William Hogarth** the 18th century painter, engraver and satirist who was born in London and lived and worked in

36

In the National: Impressionism of Georges Seurat's 'Bathers'

the capital all his life. **Gallery 7** has pictures by **William Blake** who produced weird and wonderful illustrations for poetry and the Bible in Gothic style; **Gallery 10** shows **Constable's** paintings of English landscapes; **Gallery 15**, the pre-Raphaelite Brotherhood and its followers including **Millais'** *Ophelia* and **Rossetti's** *Proserpine*. In the Modern **Galleries 30-32** are works by **Degas, Manet, Utrillo, van Gogh, Pissarro, Toulouse-Lautrec** particularly his

delightful *Les Deux Amies* and one of **Paul Cézanne's** last paintings *The Gardener*.

LUNCH: The Rex Whistler Room, the gallery's restaurant, serves delicious English food, particularly the selection of cheeses, in a pretty basement dominated by a colourful mural 'The Expedition in Pursuit of Rare Meats' by Whistler. The wine list is excellent - half bottles a speciality. Booking is

In the National: the symbolism of Jan van Eyck's 'The Arnolfini Marriage'

37

usually essential (834 6754). Those who prefer to press on with the tour and spend less should head for the coffee shop which is self-service with an array of salads and sandwiches.

Leave the Tate Gallery by the main entrance turning right along Millbank towards Vauxhall Bridge Road and *Pimlico* underground. Take the Victoria line three stops to *Oxford Circus*.

Leave by *Regent Street North* exit, walk straight ahead and, a short way along, take the third left into Cavendish Place continuing into Wigmore Street. Turn right at Duke Street into Manchester Square and opposite is Hertford House, the **Wallace Collection**.

The Marquesses of Hertford's London home contains a collection of porcelain, furniture and paintings, even armoury, all on show in rooms once used by this wealthy French-English family.

Portraits of the Hertfords are in the ground-floor lobby. The iron and bronze balustrade of the staircase is decorated with the royal monogram of French kings. It was bought as scrap from the old Palais Mazarin in Paris.

Go up to the landing with some fine paintings by **Boucher** and turn left to **Room 13** with paintings by **Canaletto** and **Guardi**.

In **Room 14** among the beautiful pieces of furniture and porcelain, is the **Régulateur Clock** with elaborate astronomical movements showing sunrise and sunset. The case is in oak inlaid with purple and tulip wood. It was made in France. A Louis XV musical clock

Turner at the Tate: the tranquil evening landscape of 'Chichester Canal'

38

Eating out at the Tate: a detail from 'Pursuit of Rare Meats' by Whistler

is on the mantelpiece. In the centre showcases are fine collections of Sèvres porcelain in dark blue and in green and pink.

Head back through **Room 13**, turn left and walk through **Rooms 15 to 18**, hung with exquisite 17th century Dutch cabinet pictures, to enter the main picture gallery, **Room 19**, described as one of the finest in the world.

Here are seventy paintings of the 17th century including ones by Rembrandt, Velázquez, Rubens, van Dyck, Titian, Poussin and Claude. Straight ahead is **Titian's** *Perseus and Andromeda*, **Poussin's** *A Dance to the Music of Time*, two full-length portraits by **van Dyck**, *Rainbow Landscape* by **Rubens** and **Velázquez'** famous portrait *Lady with a Fan*.

Also, works by **Murillo** including *Adoration of the Shepherds* and **Rubens'** *Holy Family with St Elizabeth and John the Baptist*.

On the south wall are Dutch pictures including the famous *Laughing Cavalier* by **Frans Hals** - not laughing, more an enigmatic smile. Also a moving portrait by **Rembrandt** of his son Titus.

For a final gallery, go out into the square, across to Duke Street and turn left at Oxford Street for *Bond Street* underground.

Take the Jubilee Line two stops to *Charing Cross*. Pick up the exit signs for *The Strand*, walk along on the right past The Savoy hotel, cross the approach to Waterloo Bridge and **Somerset House** is on the right. It was built in the Palladian style at the end of the 18th century. Queen Elizabeth I lived here for a time.

The **Courtauld Institute Galleries** occupy eleven rooms in the north wing. Part of the east wing is used by the University of London's Kings College. The collection includes Impressionist and post-Impressionist paintings and other works of art bequeathed by industrialist Samuel Courtauld. Also shown is the most recent addition, the Count Antoine Seilern bequest of paintings and drawings by Rubens and Michelangelo.

This is how the paintings are displayed: in **Galleries 1-2** Renaissance and Rubens; **Gallery 3** Rubens; and **Gallery 4** Tiepolo.

In **Galleries 5-6** are the French Impressionist and post-Impressionist works. They include **Cézanne's** *Cardplayers*, **Degas'** *Two Dancers on the Stage*, **Gaugin's** *Nevermore*, **Manet's** *Déjeuner sur l'Herbe* and *Bar at the Folies-Bergère*, **Modigliani's** *Nude*, **Renoir's** *La Loge*, **Pissarro's** *Lordship Lane Station*, **Seurat's** *Young Woman at a Powder Table*, **Toulouse-Lautrec's** *Jean Avril* and **van Gogh's** *Portrait of the Artist with Bandaged Ear*.

In **Gallery 7** are 18th and 19th century portraits and Chambers' Medal Cabinet plus Huguenot silver; **Gallery 8** - the Great Room - a display for lectures; **Gallery 9-10** 20th century paintings; and **Gallery 11** Italian and Dutch art from the 13th-15th century.

TEA: Enjoy tea or coffee in the gallery cafe. Or return along the Strand to The Savoy for an afternoon tea in the elegant Thames Foyer room of this grand hotel with a piano or harp as background. Finger sandwiches with brown or white bread, scones, pastries, small éclairs and a choice of teas.

Tonight, a show. There are fifty theatres in the West End at the

40

Smiling not 'Laughing Cavalier'

41

'Two Dancers on the Stage': a close-up by Degas in the Courtauld

last count. The *Evening Standard* newspaper lists places and times and the weekly magazine *Time Out* has reviews as well.

DINNER: For a pre-theatre, good value meal, there is the family-run Food for Thought in an old banana warehouse in Neal Street, Covent Garden (unlicensed, closes at 20.00). This venerable cafe provides vegetarian dishes such as shepherdess pie, cauliflower Lyonnaise and smoked tofu and

alfalfa salad followed by straw-berry and chocolate scrunch.

Before or after the show, Porters in Henrietta Street nearby serves really traditional English food - pies, stews and fishcakes, followed by bread and butter pudding.

Or, for French flavour, Cafe des Amis du Vin, Hanover Place, off Long Acre - a brasserie-style restaurant on the ground floor, a winebar in the basement and an elegant restaurant on the first floor. ❑

The celebrity crowd

**Henry VIII presents the wife, Prince Edward introduces himself,
Cliff Richard moves it, Gielgud makes his mark
and Ronnie Scott improvises**

It's people that make London. Not only kings and queens but film stars, artists, writers and all those Londoners who help set the trend for their period of history. Many of these personalities are re-created at **Madame Tussaud's** waxworks, one of London's most popular tourist attractions.

Arrive early - just after 09.00. The nearest underground station is *Baker Street*. Turn left at the top of the steps, past the distinctive dome of the Planetarium to the entrance along Marylebone Road.

Madame Tussaud arrived in London in 1802 with unusual items in her luggage - death masks of those beheaded at the time of the French Revolution. She had made these for her father's waxworks

exhibition and for thirty years she travelled around Britain showing them and adding new figures.

Her first permanent exhibition opened in Baker Street in 1835. She died in 1850 and her sons moved Tussaud's to the present site in 1884. In 1925 the building was destroyed by fire but the moulds were saved and the museum reopened three years later. Moulds are made from a sculpted original. Eyes, hair and colour are added once the wax head is cast. Many people donate their own clothes to ensure accuracy. Moulds are used again when the wax deteriorates.

The fun of touring Madame Tussaud's is being deceived by the wax policemen and doormen dotted here and there. Their directions

42

are not essential as the only route is well signposted. There are also debates about the likeness or otherwise of different figures.

This is not the case in the first section which re-creates scenes from British history and literature. After all, who knows what **Guy Fawkes** or the poor **Princes in the Tower** really looked like? But once into the **Conservatory** there is a host of famous faces. These are constantly changed to keep up to date with television programmes, films and the news.

The **Grand Hall**, magnificently refurbished with chandeliers and gilt mouldings, is a different matter. On display is a series of historic figures starting with a re-creation of **Marie-Antoinette's** boudoir at the Palace of Versailles and the royal family sculpted from life by Madame Tussaud herself. Other French kings and queens, portrayed by Madame Tussaud and her successors, follow thick and fast. The group of **Henry VIII and**

his six wives is one of the most impressive tableaux in the Grand Hall. The figures, researched from paintings and written descriptions, were completed in 1984.

The modern-day **British royal family** group is equally striking. Positioned strategically at the top of the room, the family is surrounded by royalty from other countries and **politicians** - new faces are added at frequent intervals.

From here, go down into the **Chamber of Horrors** where, as well as Madame Tussaud's original deathmasks, there are villains, murderers and murder scenes.

The re-enactment of the **Battle of Trafalgar** is a fitting conclusion, with its dramatic ending as Lord Nelson draws his last breath at the height of victory.

COFFEE: Take coffee at the Legends Cafe with the famous - all waxworks, of course.

Leave the exhibition, turning right for *Baker Street* station. Take 43

Ronnie Scott's Club, Soho

COVENT GARDEN

Theatre Museum

St. Paul's, Church

Waterloo Bridge

Hungerford Bridge

THAMES

Museum of the Moving Image

the underground direct to *Piccadilly Circus* and follow signs for *London Pavilion*. This handsome white building fronting the Circus, with an original façade of 1885, has had a chequered history. Originally a music hall, it became a theatre in 1918 and cinema in 1934. It was closed for several years before being rebuilt as part of **Trocadero Shopping Centre**.

Take the escalator to **London Pavilion's Rock Circus**, modern technology linked to waxworks. Put on headsets at the entrance and meet fifty wax models re-creating thirty years of pop music history including **Bill Haley and the Comets**, the four **Beatles** playing together again and **Elton John**. All are seen and heard performing - stand in front of them and the hits of each artist are played through the headset. If pop music and electronics are a turn off, explore the shops in the arcades instead.

44   Back into **Piccadilly Circus**. This is the heart of London; take in the scene - traffic whirling round one side of the famous **Eros** statue, the colourful neon advertising and the hustle and bustle of people from all over the world.

The statue was first unveiled in 1893 and soon became known as Eros. It is not Eros at all, but the *Angel of Charity* modelled by Sir Alfred Gilbert as a memorial to the philanthropist Lord Shaftesbury. Eros was moved to the south side of the Circus in 1986 for easier pedestrian access.

Walk along Coventry Street to **Leicester Square** - surrounded by cinemas and restaurants. On the right is the **Half Price Ticket Booth** which sells theatre tickets for the same night's performances at half price. Shows on offer are displayed on a board outside.

Continue past the **Empire**, a spot for late-night dancing and, further along on the corner, is the **Hippodrome** now a hi-tech disco, once an Edwardian music hall.

Cross Charing Cross Road with theatres to the right, into Cranbourn Street, over St Martin's Lane with several more and along Long Acre to *Covent Garden* underground.

LUNCH: Turn left into Neal Street and at the first junction, on the right, is Antonio Carluccio's up-market Neal Street Restaurant. His style of Italian cooking and in particular his enthusiasm for mushrooms have made him an author and television star. Booking is essential (836 8368). Just opposite in a converted ware-house, is the restaurants and art galleries complex owned by

Tussaud's: Edward meets Edward ...

and a line-up of the famous

Christina Smith. The basement restaurant carrying her name provides an excellent daily menu from mid-day to 23.30 or less elaborate meals in the winebar. For snacks there is her Cafe Casbar next door in Earlham Street.

Alternatively, at Covent Garden underground station, turn into James Street and left for Bertorelli's at 44a Floral Street. Ex-London University students have fond memories of this restaurant name, now a chic, Italian cafe run by a grandson. Choose lunch in the Ristorante or pizza, pasta or salads in the winebar below.

Return to James Street, at the side of *Covent Garden* station. On the left is the back of the **Royal Opera House** now being extended.

This is the heart of **Covent Garden**, once the site of London's main vegetable, fruit and flower markets. Turn right and left to stand by the portico of **St Paul's** - the actors' church and the setting for the opening scene of the musical *My Fair Lady*. It is now the stage for a succession of buskers and street theatre.

Inspired by his travels in Italy, architect Inigo Jones designed the square as a piazza, surrounding it with colonnaded town houses. It was the biggest open place in 17th century London.

Market stalls soon appeared; coffee houses, so popular in the 18th century, were established; and flower-sellers strolled around the square approaching people as they spilled out of the old Royal Opera House which had its entrance in the corner of the piazza.

Market halls replaced the wooden booths and stalls. In 1830 the **Central Market** was opened, the iron and glass roof was added fifty years later. In 1872 the **Flower Market** in the far corner was built and the **Jubilee Hall** for exotic fruits in 1908.

The huge wholesale market operation which developed created its own problems - enormous traffic jams in the early morning and a deserted area for the rest of the day. In 1974 the market was moved to the other side of the Thames. Plans to raze Covent Garden and replace it with offices were overturned. Market buildings were refurbished and the piazza is now a popular shopping and entertainment centre.

Continue round the piazza, through the middle of the market with cafes, stalls and shops; then head for the old Flower Market in the corner. The **Theatre Museum**, entrance in Russell Street, shares this old market building with the London Transport Museum which re-creates 150 years of public transport in the capital.

The Theatre Museum has on show theatre memorabilia and archives assembled by the Victoria and Albert Museum over eighty years. The entrance opens up into a large foyer with several exhibits

---

Round and about the capital

London's transport system works well. For the visitor, the underground is the best bet, trains are comfortable - other than in rush hours - and directions and maps are easy to understand.

The Seven Day Travel Card makes getting about simpler and cheaper. Take along a passport-sized photograph to any station. A Zone One card is sufficient.

Cards can be used for the red buses, a more pleasant way to see the city, particularly from the top deck, if only routes were easier to understand and traffic did not make journey times uncertain.

Drivers of that other traditional sight, the black taxi-cabs, had to pass 'the knowledge', a test on every byway of the capital, before being given a licence. Only hail cabs with the yellow 'taxi' sign lit - it means they are for hire. ❑

including the statue of **Spirit of Gaiety** from the Gaiety Theatre and the **original box office** from the old Duke of York's Theatre. The ornate **circle box**, with occupants in Victorian dress, was from the Glasgow Palace.

A long ramp takes the visitor to the lower level. Set into the walls on both sides are **hand-prints** of the stars including Peggy Ashcroft, John Gielgud and Rex Harrison.

To the right is a **theatre bar** with theatrical portraits. On the left, the **history of theatre** is re-created in display cases, following the time sequence from the early days of puppetry and circus to today's musicals and pop shows. Costumes, make-up, posters and programmes are part of the display with voices of the famous.

There are special exhibitions on theatrical themes such as costume design, photography or the life of a well-known thespian. In the museum's theatre, there are regular performances by actors and actresses, auditions by drama schools and lectures by celebrities.

TEA: In a replica bandstand is the museum's fascinating cafe. Stage props, lighting desks and sound effects machines are a suitable setting for Earl Grey with Millionaire's shortbread or dark chocolate cake and cream.

From the world of the theatre move into that of films - unless it is Monday when the next venue is closed. Turn right out of the exit in Russell Street and right into Bow Street. Further over in Catherine Street is the legendary Theatre Royal, Drury Lane.

Walk past the Lyceum on the right, once a famous theatre. Cross the Strand for Waterloo Bridge. Stop on the bridge for the view of the river - one of the best in London because of the way the river bends.

Once across the River, take the steps on the right to the entrance of the **Museum of Moving Image**.

There are 'Pacing Yourself' posters at regular intervals with a plan and a list of exhibits still to come - a good idea as it is easy to get caught up. The first part of the exhibition looks at the development of film from optical experiments *Fantasmagorie* to *Phenakistoscope* with an opportunity to experience these as well as follow the work of pioneers such as Lumière. Bring coins for the *Kinetoscope* machines with pictures of 'naughty ladies'.

The section **The Early Years** features Hollywood and one of the most spectacular exhibits **Temple of the Gods**. Statues of 'silent' stars support a frieze dedicated to Charlie Chaplin while the ceiling pays tribute to a host of early idols. With a back-cloth of an East End shop front, where Chaplin was born, 'Penny Shows' can be watched with excerpts from his *The Immigrant*.

Early Soviet cinema is on view in a railway carriage with one of the many real-life actor-guides playing the rôle of revolutionary. From a

46

Central Hall, Covent Garden: peace in the early morning

Re-created: the spirit of London's theatre

set looking out over the rooftops of Paris, excerpts from famous French films can be seen.

Cinema comes of age with **The Talkies** starting with Al Jolson and *The Jazz Singer* of 1927. **Drawings that Walk and Talk** picks up characters from Micky Mouse to Tom and Jerry and children can draw their own, helped by a resident animator.

The golden age of Hollywood with its lavish musicals, westerns and special effects is illustrated in **The Hollywood Dream Factory**. In the museum's studio, a director is casting for his next film and visitors can take part in front of or behind the camera. Also watch excerpts from 500 major movies - all in six minutes. A gold-braided commissionaire in the Art Deco foyer of the Muswell Hill Odeon introduces **Made in Britain** and a uniformed usherette explains home-grown films from *The Lavender Hill Mob* to *Chariots of Fire*.

Television now becomes the centre of attraction with a choice of nine screens showing excerpts from soap-operas to newscasts and early commercials. In a television studio, visitors can 'fly' superimposed over London, or do a 'live' news report.

A **Fantastic Voyages** section from *2001: A Space Odyssey* in 1968 to *ET* in 1982 with 'pods' from *Alien*

and costumes from the epic *Star Wars* creates a futuristic climax.

To return, walk in front of the Royal Festival Hall and cross the river at Hungerford Bridge by the footbridge along the railway to the *Embankment* underground station on the other side.

DINNER: Seeing the famous continues this evening. Book for a star-name concert at the Royal Festival Hall - dinner before or after in the Review Restaurant (921 0800) with French-style cuisine, over-looking the river, or the buffet in the foyer.

For an informal evening there is jazz at Pizza on the Park, Knightsbridge, near Hyde Park Corner. Short-stay jazz names are in the Jazz Room downstairs. Eat there or in the restaurant. Bookings taken for both the 21.15 and 23.15 jazz sessions (235 5550).

Or take the opportunity to meet Britain's own legendary jazzman Ronnie Scott at his club in the heart of Soho, 47 Frith Street (439 0747). There are usually two groups. Every world jazz star has played this venue at some time. Meals are served from 20.30, jazz from 21.30 until 03.00. ❏

Reflections in the water

Sailing past a wartime sloop, saluting the Mayflower, climbing aboard a tea clipper, marking the Meridian at Greenwich and riding a space-age train through Docklands

London's history is reflected in its rivers and it is the Thames that provides the city's origins. The river was the route to the sea and, because of this asset, the capital dominated the rest of the nation.

By Tudor times, London's cloth exports constituted three-quarters of the country's overseas trade. In much the same way, corn growers of Cambridgeshire, dairy farmers of Suffolk and graziers of the Midlands all looked to London as the hub of their universe.

The Roman settlement of Londinium, where wharves were built along the river to create a port, has become the largest city in the world. Each day, more people use Waterloo railway station on the banks of the Thames than travel on all the railways of the United States. The River Thames is the focus for today. Reflected in its waters will be the Embankment, the South Bank centre, St Paul's, the towers of the City and the Barbican, the Tower of London and Greenwich, ten kilometres downstream. Then there is a ride on a light railway through Docklands.

Take the tube to *Westminster*, walk the subway to Westminster Pier to arrive for the first boat which leaves at 10.30. Buy a single ticket for Greenwich. The standard of comfort on boats varies but they all have an indoor, heated area, toilets and refreshments. Some boats provide commentaries - not always accurate but often amusing. It is difficult to say exactly how long

48

the trip will take, as it depends on the tide; estimate for anything from forty-five minutes to one hour.

Westminster Pier is situated opposite **County Hall**, once the seat of the Greater London Council, abolished in 1986.

Setting off downstream, the first landmark is the **South Bank Arts Complex** on the right which includes the Royal Festival Hall, Queen Elizabeth Hall, the Hayward Gallery and the National Theatre.

On the opposite bank of the river **Cleopatra's Needle**, the 3,500 year-old Egyptian obelisk, is strikingly positioned. The tour boat then passes under the modern **Waterloo Bridge**. The beautiful building set back from the Embankment on the left after the bridge is **Somerset House,** home of the Courtauld Institute Galleries. Further along is the historic **Temple** - a group of legal colleges and chambers going back to the Middle Ages.

Permanently moored along the Embankment here is the *HQS Wellington*, a world war two escort vessel and the only floating Livery Hall - the meeting place of the Honourable Company of Master Mariners. Further along is *The President*, a world war one sloop, now owned by a charity, once the headquarters of the Royal Naval Volunteer Reserve.

There is a fine view of **St Paul's Cathedral** from this stretch of the river. On the right between **Blackfriars** and **Southwark bridges** and next to the massive **Bankside Power Station** is where the American actor/producer Sam Wanamaker is spearheading the new **Shakespeare Globe Theatre**.

London Bridge usually comes as something of a disappointment - it is completely unremarkable, unlike its early predecessor which had shops and houses on it.

Left is the old **Billingsgate Fish Market** now commercial offices; next to it is the **Custom House**, where ships moored in the Pool of London, as this part of the river is called, used to 49

Docklands Light Railway

The Mayflower

Cutty Sark

Pedestrian Tunnel

Zero Meridian Longitude

National Maritime Museum

GREENWICH

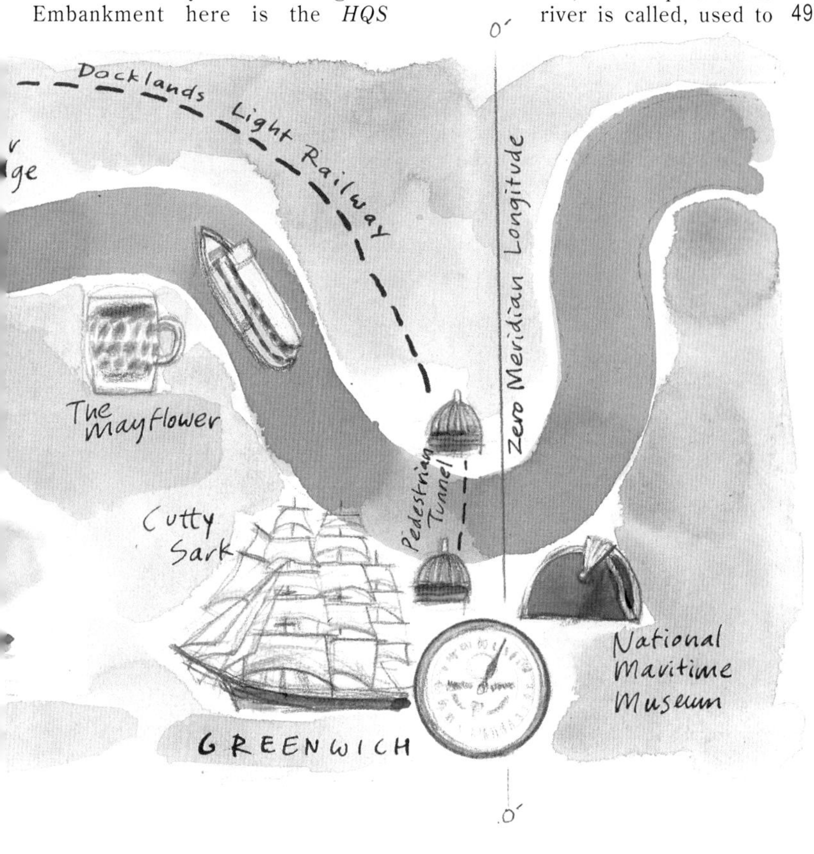

pay their dues. These days most freight is unloaded much further down at Tilbury or at coastal ports.

Further on is **Tower Bridge**, a symbol of London and the last bridge before the sea. The middle part of the bridge opens to let through large ships which moor alongside *HMS Belfast* on the right, a wartime cruiser now a museum. Opposite is the striking outline of the White Tower and the other buildings of the **Tower of London**.

Docklands starts after Tower Bridge with **St Katharine's Dock** on the left and the **World Trade Centre**. On the opposite side of the river is **Butler's Wharf** a new development of an old brewery and wharves which includes workshops, flats, a hotel and, in a startling white building, the **Design Museum**.

Look left again to the restyled wharves and among them the 17th century **Town of Ramsgate** pub. On the south bank, look out for the **Angel pub** and then at Rotherhithe the **Mayflower** - an 18th century pub named after the ship of the Pilgrim Fathers who left here on their north-Atlantic voyage to settle in North America. The captain of the *Mayflower* is buried in the nearby churchyard. Further along, on the opposite bank, among luxury flats in converted warehouses is the **Prospect of Whitby** - a docks pub

50

with a history going back to 1520, now with music every night.

On the left is **Limehouse**, again with major redevelopments transforming what was once a seedy docks area known as Chinatown.

The boat travels in a large loop as the river swings round the **Isle of Dogs** on the north bank. This is the location for most of Docklands development which will be better appreciated from the return journey on the Docklands Light Railway.

On the south bank is **Deptford** where royal naval ships were once built; then **Greenwich** with its graceful buildings - the Royal Naval College, the National Maritime Museum and, at the top of the hill, the Old Royal Observatory. On the quayside in a dry dock is the **Cutty Sark**, built in 1869 and one of the last sailing clippers to carry tea from China.

COFFEE: At the pier is a small cafe for passengers who prefer their coffee on dry land.

A stroll round the covered crafts market in the town centre will take up time if necessary before the later midday opening of the *Cutty Sark* on a Sunday.

The area in front of the pier is called **Cutty Sark Gardens** and on the left is the *Cutty Sark*. Climb

Prospect of Whitby: sing-along among the apartments

51

Cutty Sark: once carrying tea from China

aboard and go below deck to admire forty spectacular carved and painted figureheads from other ships of the period - the largest collection in the world. Afterwards, walk on deck to the fo'c'sle to inspect the cramped crew quarters and the galley where meals were cooked on a coal-fired range. Below, in the bows, is a pen for animals. Ships like the *Cutty Sark* carried a pig and chickens to eke out the diet of salt meat, beans and biscuits.

Across the Gardens is the yacht **Gipsy Moth IV** used by Sir Francis Chichester in 1966-1967 to sail round the world single-handed.

LUNCH: There are many pubs and restaurants in Greenwich. The historic Trafalgar Tavern, two minutes walk downstream along the river bank, combines a square meal with a taste of history. Dickens and his friends used to arrive by boat.

The bar, with a section for children, has good sandwiches, **rolls and bar snacks. In the restaurant, traditional English dishes are served. 'Musts' are the house specialities, Trafalgar devilled whitebait to start and hot cherries and ice cream to finish. In between, traditional roast beef, chicken or steaks. Best to book: 858 2507.**

After lunch a walk in the park. Along Park Row, across the busy Romney Road, then through Park Row Gate into **Greenwich Park**.

This was once a royal hunting ground and Henry VIII and both his daughters Mary and Elizabeth were born at the palace which stood where the Royal Naval College is now and spent much of their childhood here. The trunk of an oak tree where the future Queen Elizabeth I played as a child survives. The park is still a royal park with an area of 'wilderness' where a flock of deer roams - mostly out of sight.

Head up the steep path to the **Old Royal Observatory**. This is a group of buildings established in 1675 when Wren built **Flamsteed House** as the living and working quarters for the first royal astronomer. Other buildings were added including a small planetarium in the **South Building**. The Red Time Ball on top of Flamsteed House drops at 13.00 every day. It was installed in 1833 to help ships on the Thames set chronometers. This is where Greenwich Mean Time started and the first Meridian '0' was drawn. As the air became polluted and the skies too 'light' from artificial sources, the Royal Observatory moved to Sussex.

Walk inside the Old Royal Observatory to find out more about astronomy. Start by crossing the Meridian in the courtyard where numerous people are photographed with a leg in each hemisphere. Enter Flamsteed House and the 17th century living rooms set up as they would have been when the first astronomer Flamsteed lived here.

Cross the garden to **Meridian House** to see huge astronomical instruments used by Flamsteed and his successors, Halley, Bradley and Airy to define the Meridian. Further on are early chronometers and a display on the history of time and time-keeping. It is hard to imagine, but towns in Britain all had their own time. In the end they were united by the railway - they had to agree on a timetable.

On leaving the observatory,

Cube Room: spiralling tulips

pause to admire the spectacular view of London - the Thames, the Isle of Dogs with its rising tower blocks and in the distance Tower Bridge, even National Westminster Tower and St Paul's on a clear day.

Down the hill on the left is the **National Maritime Museum**. This splendid set of buildings includes **Queen's House** - join a guided tour to see this attractive Palladian villa designed by Inigo Jones. Recently refurbished, the room settings are as close to the original as possible. Particularly beautiful is the main hall, the **Cube Room**, a perfect cube 40 foot by 40 foot by 40 foot. It has a decorated ceiling, matching floor and spiral staircase with a tulip motif on its iron balusters.

Into the museum and **Neptune Hall** to see the Paddle Tug *Reliant* a steam ship built in 1907 with its engines and cabins set up as they would have been at the time. From here enter **Royal Barge House** and admire the splendid-looking craft which carried the royal family to and from the royal palaces at Hampton Court, Whitehall, the Tower and Greenwich. In **Gallery 9** is Nelson's coat with its bullet hole, This is on view among a series of exhibits commemorating the great admiral. Turner's painting of the Battle of Trafalgar sets the scene for the fatal bullet.

TEA: Sit down with a cup of tea in the museum cafe before continuing to the Royal Naval College, closing at 17.00.

From the museum cross the road to the **Royal Naval College**. Designed by Sir Christopher Wren as the hospital for seamen, this is a working college - Prince Andrew studied here. The **Painted Hall** is very much in use by the officers - they will have had lunch here. The magnificent ceiling was decorated by Sir James Thornhill. Opposite is the **Chapel** decorated in delicate blue, white and gold.

Walk back to the Cutty Sark Gardens and enter the dome-shaped building, entrance to the pedestrian tunnel. Descend by lift to walk

52

In original splendour: Inigo Jones' Queen's House

along the 400 metres of tunnel under the River Thames.

Emerge on the other side of the river through an identical dome-shaped building in the **Island Gardens**. Pause to look back and admire the Naval College buildings across the river before boarding **Docklands' Light Railway**.

With a ticket for *Tower Hill* board the remotely-controlled train - no driver but a Train Captain.

The overhead ride follows old train viaducts to *Crossharbour* station. Here, overlooking **Millwall Dock**, is the **London Docklands Arena** used for sporting events and concerts. It is surrounded by office blocks and workshops, among them the offices and printing works of the *Guardian* and the *Daily Telegraph* national newspapers.

The railway crosses the three basins of **West India Dock** with the most spectacular development taking place at **Canary Wharf** where three skyscrapers - one at 245 metres, the tallest building in London - are under construction with offices, flats, hotels and shops.

Right is the new **Billingsgate Fish Market**. Further on are the old London docks, mostly filled in, but **Shadwell Basin** remains with a canal through to the river. Past *Shadwell* on the left is **St George in the East** by Hawksmoor and

beyond The Highway are the offices and printing plant of News International, the site of a drawn-out dispute and pitched-battles when Rupert Murdoch's company moved here and broke the power of the printing unions in 1986.

The railway ends at **Tower Hill** from where it is just a short walk to the underground station.

The final evening of *Seven Days in London* is a return to the heart of London, Piccadilly Circus.

DINNER: Langan's is the most famous restaurant in Britain. A stylish brasserie with a friendly and cheerful atmosphere, it is a magnet for celebrities and paparazzi. Michael Caine is a partner. Start with a spinach soufflé, follow with wing of skate or roast duck with sage and onion stuffing and finish with treacle tart or delicate rice pudding. Bookings essential (491 8822). It is in Stratton Street off Piccadilly (Green Park underground station).

Or, just off Piccadilly Circus (second on the left along Shaftesbury Avenue) at No 31 Great Windmill Street is The Piccadilly. A genuine welcome, homely cooking with unusual fish and vegetarian dishes - and excellent Italian house wines.

53

Staying awhile

**For those with days to spare, an invitation to drive a train,
master a maze, cringe at the creepy-crawlies
and after a movie, munch pasta to late-night jazz**

Brass Rubbing

Britain's age of chivalry - knights in armour, costumed ladies and heraldic beasts - lives on in medieval brasses. Half an hour spent rubbing wax on paper taped over the brass can produce a memento or picture to frame. These can be created in the crypt of St Martin-in-the-Fields in Trafalgar Square (10.00-18.00, Sunday 12.00-18.00) where the brasses include 15th century Margaret Peyton, whose filigree dress has earned her the title of *The Lace Lady;* and Westminster Abbey (09.00-17.00, closed Sunday) where the 150 facsimiles range from the smallest - a Nativity scene - to the largest and oldest - Sir Robert de Bures, over two metres tall in chain mail and tabard.

British Museum   underground Tottenham Court Road
Great Russell Street

10.00-17.00 Mon-Sat   14.30-18.00 Sunday

This national museum has priceless antiquities from Assyria (now North Iraq), Egypt, Rome and Greece - including the Elgin Marbles from the Parthenon in Athens; the Sutton Hoo Treasures, jewellery and weapons from the burial ship of an AD 625 English king; and the Roman Portland Vase, the world's most precious vase dating from the time of Anthony and Cleopatra and only recently rebuilt. Its precious documents include the *Magna Carta*, the last diary notes of Captain Scott of the Antarctic and Lord Nelson, Leonardo da Vinci's sketch book and the medieval *Lindisfarne Gospels*.

The entrance from Montague Place leads to the huge attic where the museum has bowed to inevitable demand and opened a Japanese gallery to display its collection, the best in Europe. At the entrance, in austere Japanese style timber work, is a case displaying hundreds of examples of the art of Netsuke - miniature sculptures - and inside the gallery are Japanese paintings, pottery, porcelain, screens and prints of the Ukiyoe school. Centrepiece is a setting of a Japanese tea-house ceremony created in every detail by the Keeper of Japanese Antiquities, Lawrence Smith. Once a month the actual ceremony is staged with a genuine Tea Master.

Cinemas

More than two hundred films are shown in London every week. The major releases are best seen in the large West End cinemas grouped mainly around Leicester Square: the Leicester Square Theatre; the Odeon, frequently used for British premieres; and Empires 1 and 2. Other large screen cinemas are the Canons in Shaftesbury Avenue and Haymarket; Odeon Marble Arch; and the Plaza Lower Regent Street. Smaller, specialized cinemas include:

Curzon Phoenix, Charing Cross Road
Curzon West End, Shaftesbury Avenue
Curzon Mayfair, Curzon Street

Owned by a film distribution company that prides itself on the quality of its movies - and cinemas. Three outlets, all luxurious, plenty of leg room, coffee, licensed bar in the first two. Films are foreign with subtitles unless own English productions.

Gate Cinema, Notting Hill Gate
Not mainstream but first-run films, divided equally between English language and foreign, with sub-titles. Monday to Saturday separate performances. Sunday matinées with classic revivals or double-bills.

Covent Garden   underground Covent Garden
The Royal Opera House
Bow Street

The present theatre opened in 1858 and except for a break during the two world wars, has included opera and ballet in its productions ever since. Caruso and Dame Nellie Melba sang here and the Russian Ballet of Sergei Diaghilev gave its first performance in England in 1911. Placido Domingo, Kiri te Kanawa and Pavarotti are regular visitors. It was renamed the Royal Opera House in 1892. The Sadler's Wells Ballet was transferred to Covent Garden and retitled The Royal Ballet by charter from the Queen in 1956. The opera company received a similar award in 1968. There are a few seats available on the day from the booking office in Floral Street, one per person.

55

Design museum: quality of life

Design Museum   underground Tower Hill
Butler's Wharf   ferry from Tower Pier
Shad Thames
(south east side of Tower Bridge)
11.30-18.30 closed Monday

From chairs to coffee makers, telephones to typewriters - how design contributes to the quality of life. There are three sections: **Review** exhibits the latest fashions including the futuristic Nissan S-cargo car; **Study Collection** on the top floor is a history of 20th century design with now-treasured nostalgia such as a 1930s Pye wireless receiver, Peter Behrens' 1909 electric kettle, Alvar Aalto furniture and a 1928 Tetra model car designed by Le Corbusier; and the third section is **Boilerhouse**, illustrating topical themes. The museum, created by Sir Terence Conran, also has a graphics exhibition area and a library of books, journals and slides. The riverside cafe serves snacks and the restaurant lunches and dinners.

FLORENCE NIGHTINGALE MUSEUM

Florence Nightingale Museum   underground Waterloo
within the grounds of St Thomas' Hospital
2 Lambeth Palace Road
10.00-16.00 closed Monday

This museum is devoted to the life of Florence Nightingale, 'The Lady with the Lamp' who tended sick and injured British troops in the 1850s during the war against Russia in the Crimea and campaigned all her life for improved nursing care.

On display are: the childhood books of her privileged and comfortable early years; William Russell's wartime despatches in *The Times* about her work at the hospital in Scutari where, against indifference, she and her small band of nurses improved conditions on the wards and operating theatres and reduced the death rate from 42% to 2.2%; and her work on returning to Britain in setting up the first school of nursing in 1860. Centrepiece of the museum is a life-size re-creation of the ward at Scutari.

Geffrye Museum   underground Old Street
Kingsland Road
10.00-17.00 Tues-Sat 14.00-17.00 Sunday

Set in a furniture-making district of east London and housed in 18th century almshouses, this museum - named after a 17th century Lord Mayor - tells the fascinating story of the British front room. Nine rooms with paintings and ornaments re-create the oak furniture and panelling of Elizabethan and Stuart times, the walnut of the William and Mary decades, painted pine and mahogany furniture of Georgian taste through to the mass production and cluttered look of the Victorians and the Art Nouveau and Art Deco styles of earlier this century. There is a coffee bar and adjoining gardens.

Hampton Court Palace   rail Waterloo to Hampton Court
East Molesey
09.30-18.00 mid-March - mid-October
09.30-16.30 mid-October - mid-March

Thirty-two kilometres upstream on the Thames, this palace was built by Cardinal Wolsey and enlarged by Henry VIII. The last monarch to live here was George II although there are 'grace and favour' apartments designated by the Queen. In the State and Private apartments can be seen the carvings of Grinling Gibbons, the design of Sir John Vanburgh and wrought ironwork of Jean Tijou. Outside, there is the famous maze, the largest vine in England (planted in 1768) and the Tudor tennis court where Real Tennis is played.

Keats House   underground Hampstead
Wentworth Place, Keats Grove
Hampstead
14.00-18.00 Mon-Fri April-October 13.00-17.00 Mon-Fri November-March
10.00-13.00 14.00-17.00 Saturday 14.00-17.00 Sunday

This house where the romantic poet Keats lived was saved from demolition in the early 1920s by donations, largely from America. When Keats lived there, for two years from 1819, Hampstead was a secluded village and this inspired *Ode to a Nightingale* as well as five of his other great odes. It was here he fell in love with Fanny Brawne, a neighbour's daughter and his early death at twenty-six came shortly after they had become engaged. The house retains the original windows and shutters, the shelves on which he kept his books and an extensive collection of his manuscripts and letters and those of his friends and contemporaries, among them Shelley and Wordsworth.

56

Kew Gardens: Chinese folly among the rhododendrons

Kensington Palace   **underground High Street, Kensington**
The Broad Walk
Kensington Gardens

09.00-17.00 Mon-Sat   13.00-17.00 Sunday

The wedding of the last decade was that of the Prince and Princess of Wales.
The beautiful silk dress worn by the Princess on 29 July, 1981 can be seen
here in the Court Dress Collection, a dazzling display of dresses and uniforms
spanning twelve reigns and shown in period room settings. The palace has
been a royal residence since 1689 and the Prince and Princess and Princess
Margaret live in private apartments beyond the state rooms. Wren redesigned
the house for King William III since when many great artists, including
Grinling Gibbons and William Kent, have enhanced the building. The formal
State Apartments with fine paintings, furniture and gifts include the room in
which Queen Victoria is believed to have been born. Outside the palace is
Kensington Gardens with its famous Round Pond and statue of Peter Pan, J
M Barrie's well-loved children's character, the boy who never grew up.

Kew Gardens (Royal Botanic)   **underground Kew Gardens**
Kew, Richmond

09.30 to dusk

These world-famous gardens receive more than a million visitors a year and
the numbers are increasing. Attractions are not just the 50,000 plants but
also the follies and temples, notably the Chinese Pagoda, built in 1761; the
Marianne North flower paintings; the Temperate House, a Victorian
conservatory; and the 1987 Princess of Wales Conservatory with ten different
tropical and sub-tropical habitats. Among the 2,500 species inside are rain
forest orchids, carnivorous plants and desert cacti. The Palm House is the
garden's most important building. Constructed between 1844 and 1848 by

Richard Turner in collaboration with architect Decimus Burton it is the finest surviving 19th century glass and iron structure and the most beautiful building of its type in the world. Through the second half of the 1980s, it was dismantled and rebuilt piece-by-piece. Sixteen kilometres of stainless steel glazing bars replaced the corroded Victorian metal work and 16,000 panes of curved, toughened glass were fitted into the patched original frame. In a new extended basement, there is a marine display featuring a mangrove swamp and coral reef. With the threatened loss of habitats, particularly in the rain forests, the restored Palm House is helping to save many rare and exotic species from extinction.

Music

Almost a thousand bands play live in London every week. Jazz, folk and rock clubs are to be found around Soho and Covent Garden. Many are for members but guests are welcome for a small increase in ticket price. *Time Out*, the listings magazine goes on sale every Wednesday with details and programmes for the week ahead. Sample venues:

100 Club, 100 Oxford Street
Long-established basement club, friendly atmosphere, live trad/mod, even rhythm and blues.

Rock Garden, 6-7 The Piazza, Covent Garden
Another long-time basement club, rock bands, often star names. Ring 240-3961 for daily listings.

Pizza Express, 10 Dean Street, Soho
Eat pizza in the restaurant, then go down into the jazz cellar for usually mainstream bands with star guests. Or eat while you listen.

Cafe de Paris, 3 Coventry Street
Elegant, Edwardian surroundings - every type of music and every type of dancer. Join in or watch from the balcony with a meal.

Natural History Museum　　　　　**underground South Kensington**
Cromwell Road
South Kensington

10.00-18.00 Mon-Sat　13.00-18.00 Sunday

Huge skeleton dinosaurs lurk behind the cathedral doors of this Victorian building. This is the home of the national collection of living and fossil animals, insects and plants, rocks and minerals. The scale of nature can be seen in the galleries around the central hall from the blue whale which can grow to over thirty-three metres long to microscopic algae. From a dinosaur footprint about 135 million years old to the threatened species of today. A new display area explores the miniature world of 'creepy-crawlies' with the help of models, computers and videos and shows a giant swallowtail butterfly changing from a lurid caterpillar to elegant flying machine and a real-life ants' nest where, under a microscope, ants dash to and fro collecting leaves.

National Portrait Gallery　　　　　**underground Leicester Square**
St Martin's Place
Trafalgar Square

10.00-17.00 Mon to Fri　10.00-18.00 Saturday　14.00-18.00 Sunday

This collection, founded in 1856, illustrates British social and cultural history. Portraits are arranged in chronological order - take the lift to the top floor and work down putting faces, figures and fashions to familiar names captured by artists such as Reynolds, Hogarth, Lely and Kneller. Subjects include Henry

Natural History: changes among the creepy-crawlies

VIII, William Shakespeare, Sir Isaac Newton, Handel, Keats, Nelson and Wellington, Queen Victoria, Oscar Wilde and Henry James. Paintings of the royal family include, on the ground floor, the new and controversial portrait of the Queen Mother by twenty-three-year-old Alison Watt who won the commission as part of her John Player Portrait Award.

Public Record Office Museum   **underground Chancery Lane**
Chancery Lane
10.00-17.00 closed Saturday, Sunday

Historical events come alive through the manuscripts and records held here - the most complete of any western country. There is even a section on tracing ancestors. Subjects range from the Domesday Book, the survey undertaken by William the Conqueror in 1085; the earliest manuscript of America resulting from Sir Richard Grenville's expedition in 1585 and the letters patent founding Pennsylvania granted to William Penn in 1681.

Science Museum   **underground South Kensington**
Exhibition Road
South Kensington
10.00-18.00 Mon-Sat 11.00-18.00 Sunday

Forget the dry and stuffy science lessons of schooldays - this is a museum full of action. Start at the *Exploration of Space* and move up to the *Launch Pad* where there are levers to pull and buttons to push and then explore the other

SPEAKERS' CORNER

four floors of exhibits linked by escalators, pausing for coffee on the third.
The new Sainsbury Gallery *Food for Thought* on the first floor explains the
impact of science and technology on food and the history of medicine is
shown in the *Wellcome Museum* on the fourth.

Sir John Soane's Museum   **underground Holborn**
13 Lincoln's Inn Fields
10.00-17.00 closed Sunday, Monday

This 18th century house can be seen much as it was in the lifetime of its
owner, architect Sir John Soane. He left it endowed with his fortune to be a
museum for 'amateurs and students'. Paintings include Hogarth's two
famous series *The Rake's Progress* (eight pictures) and *The Election* (four);
Watteau's *Les Noces*; a large *Venetian Scene* by Canaletto; and *The Valley of
Aosta* by Turner. One of the principal treasures - the *Sarcophagus of Seti I*
discovered in 1817 by Belzoni in the Valley of the Kings - was bought by
Soane for £2,000 after it had been refused by the British Museum.

Speakers' Corner   **underground Marble Arch**
Marble arch, Hyde Park

This is London's 'soap box' where anyone is legally free to address the
crowds on any subject as long as it is not obscene, racist, treason or likely to
cause a breach of the peace. The oratory happens mainly on Sundays. Money
may not be demanded and loudspeakers cannot be used. The tradition was
started in the early 1800s.

60 **Transport Museum, London**   **underground Covent Garden**
Covent Garden
10.00-18.00

'Hold on tight please, move along the bus' used to be the call to passengers
from the cockney conductor as he took the fare and issued a ticket on the red
double-decker London buses - bygone days, before one-man mini buses. In
the museum, every type of London bus is on show starting with the horse-
drawn omnibuses of the late 19th century and open tops of 1910.
The building of the underground network, beginning when the trains were
steam driven, is displayed and visitors can take over the controls for a
modern-day simulated journey along the circle line.

Victoria and Albert Museum   **underground South Kensington**
Cromwell Road
10.00-17.50 Mon-Sat 14.30-17.50 Sunday

The 'V & A' is one of London's most popular museums, presenting fine and
decorative arts and containing paintings, furniture, glass, pottery, silverware
and ivories from every part of the world, particularly the once far-flung
empire. The exhibition covers eleven kilometres of galleries so a visit has to
be selective. A visit to the bookshop to pick up a free location plan is an
essential first step.

War Cabinet Rooms   **underground Westminster**
Clive Steps, King Charles Street
10.00-18.00

This was the nerve centre for the British Government and the Cabinet from
1938, just before the outbreak of world war two, to 1945. In this bunker below
the government offices at the Whitehall end of St James's Park, the Cabinet
met more than 100 times to plot against the Germans whose front line was

Transport in London: days of steam

only 160 kilometres away at Calais. Churchill's wooden chair can be seen in front of a map of the world, with two red and green lights to indicate whether London was being bombed. Along the corridor is the transatlantic telephone room with its scrambled line to President Roosevelt in the White House. 61

Wellington Museum   **underground Hyde Park Corner exit 8**
Apsley House
(north side of Hyde Park Corner)
11.00-16.30 closed Monday

The Iron Duke of Wellington lived here after more than twenty years soldiering on the battlefields of Europe and India. The beautifully-furnished rooms include the twenty-seven-metre-long Waterloo Gallery, the setting for the banquet held every 18 June to celebrate Waterloo Day. On show is the Duke's superb collection of paintings with masterpieces by Velázquez, van Dyck, Goya and Rubens. Among the military trophies are the swords carried by Wellington and Napoleon at the Battle of Waterloo and the weapons taken from the body of Tipu Sahib, son of the ruling Haidar Ali of Mysore, after the capture of Seringapatam, which led to British domination of India.

Zoo   **underground Baker Street then zoo bus (Z1)**
Regents Park
09.00-18.00 Mon-Sat 09.00-19.00 Sunday April-October
10.00-16.00 November-March

From its foundation in 1826 by Sir Stamford Raffles, the zoo has developed and progressed in its care of animals. Recent changes include the Cotton Terraces for hoofed animals, the Elephant and Rhino Pavilion, the Lion Terrace, the Snowdon Aviary where visitors can walk on an elevated walkway and watch free-flying birds and the Charles Clore Pavilion with its Moonlight World which turns day into night for the nocturnal world of bats, kiwis, dormice and spiny anteaters. Highlights include more than thirty different primates, Britain's largest aquarium and the reptile house. Feeding and bathing the animals, rides, weighing the elephants (in summer) and the children's zoo mean that cameras are essential.   ❏

People and places

To really enjoy London needs this understanding of its buildings and history and the prominent figures and artists that created its culture

Adam, Robert

1728-1792 Leaving his native Scotland after the defeat of Bonnie Prince Charlie at Culloden, Robert Adam went to Italy to study and wrote a book on the Palace of Diocletian at Spalato (now Split in Yugoslavia) which made him famous. Based in London, he became Architect of the King's Works, in essence a town planner and architect, adding to the prevailing Palladian style a number of Classical themes. Besides streets and squares, Adam interiors are superb in their proportions, and in their furnishings and ceilings. His Adelphi Terrace, on the river bank below the Strand, was the second example of environmental planning in London, Wren's plans for St Paul's and the streets around being the first.

Barbican

History is preserved here from Roman times to the blitz. Just off today's London Wall are visible remains of part of the Roman city wall. A city within a city, the Barbican houses 3,000 city workers in tall tower blocks, three named after Cromwell, Shakespeare and Lauderdale. Shakespeare, then playing in and writing plays in Southwark, married Anne Hathaway in its parish church, St Giles Cripplegate, which is on a site where a stone church was built 900 years ago. Cromwell also married here, Sir Thomas More worshipped and the blind poet Milton is buried here.

Bloomsbury Square

Better known for giving its name to the Bloomsbury Group of turn-of-the-century writers than for its architecture. It was one of the first areas west of Charing Cross to be laid out as a square in the early 18th century but its original

mansions have gone. Few of the Group, which included E M Forster, Duncan Grant and Virginia Woolf, in fact lived in the square; their homes were in the squares to the north, Russell, Woburn, Tavistock and Gordon. Gertrude Stein and her brother Leo lived at 20 Bloomsbury Square, T S Eliot worked for the publishers Faber & Faber then in Russell Square, Thomas Wolfe stayed at the Imperial Hotel in Russell Square, Ralph Waldo Emerson at 63 Southampton Row and Robert Frost lived at the Poetry Bookshop, No 35 Boswell Street from 1913 to 1926; here he became acquainted with Ezra Pound. Virginia Woolf lived for a time at 46 Gordon Square, later the home of J Maynard Keynes, and Lytton Strachey at 51 Gordon Square.

Buckingham Palace

Originally Buckingham House and built in 1703 for the Duke of Buckingham and Chandos, it has been the main home of the monarch since Queen Victoria came to the throne in 1837. The royal standard flies whenever the sovereign is in residence. George III bought it in 1761 as a dower house for Queen Charlotte, and in the reign of George IV it was remodelled and its brick walls clad in Bath Stone by John Nash. Victoria put on a new frontage and had Nash's grand entrance (Marble Arch) moved to Hyde Park because it was too narrow for the state coach. In 1912 the east front of the building was given a Classical façade of Portland stone.

It retains a country house setting, standing in parkland where the annual royal garden parties are held with up to 9,000 people entertained at a time. Buckingham Palace is not open to the public, though it is possible to visit the

Royal Mews which houses the Queen's horses, ceremonial coaches and cars; and the Queen's Gallery, exhibiting displays of art treasures from the royal collection.

Cheyne Walk

This is probably the most famous literary area of London. At 24 Cheyne Row, running north from the Walk, Thomas and Jane Carlyle lived from 1834 for forty-seven years until Thomas' death. He did much of his writing in its carefully sound-proofed study. Ralph Waldo Emerson was the first distinguished American to stay here as Carlyle's guest. Later, Oliver Wendell Holmes visited the house and found it 'much neglected'. James McNeill Whistler liked the Row very much, and stayed at No 16 (home of Dante Gabriel Rossetti); at No 96 where he painted his picture of his mother; at No 101; and at No 74 where he died. Other distinguished tenants lived in the Row: Bertrand Russell the philosopher (No 14), J M W Turner the painter (No 119), Robert Scott the Antarctic explorer (No 56) and, in Lawrence Street nearby, Henry James the novelist who moved here for the last year of his life after spending some twenty years in Rye and becoming a British citizen. Other residents included George Eliot, Elizabeth Gaskell, Charles Swinburne, George Meredith, T S Eliot as well as artist John Singer Sargent. Oscar Wilde lived in neighbouring Tite Street, as did the American painter Edwin Austin Abbey.

Churchill

1874-1965 Winston Leonard Spencer Churchill was born at Blenheim Palace, near Oxford, the great house built by Sir John Vanbrugh as the nation's thanks to John Churchill, first Duke of Marlborough, the victor against the armies of Louis XIV of France. His father Lord Randolph Churchill was the third son of the sixth Duke; his mother Jennie Jerome was the beautiful socialite daughter of a wealthy New York stockbroker and a distant cousin of the Roosevelts. Churchill was educated at Harrow School and, if his school days were unremarkable, he attended prize days with filial devotion in his later years.

One thing it did give him was the feeling for words and prose style. He trained at Sandhurst Military Academy and served as a Fourth Hussars subaltern in Egypt and India and as a war correspondent in the Boer War, where his exploits made headlines.

In 1900, he entered the House of Commons as Tory MP for Oldham but became a Liberal, to hold office as president of the Board of Trade, Home Secretary and then First Lord of the Admiralty in the Liberal government.

On the outbreak of war, he advocated a blow at the Turkish and German forces in Gallipoli in 1915, which was unsuccessful and costly in lives. He took responsibility and resigned his Cabinet post to serve as a soldier in the trenches in Flanders.

On the formation of a Conservative government in 1924, Churchill became for five years Chancellor of the Exchequer.

In the 1930s, when he was in the political wilderness, he constantly thundered against the policy of appeasing the dictators. World war two brought him back to the Admiralty - and the beginning of a close and frequent correspondence with President Franklin Delano Roosevelt.

In May 1940, he became Prime Minister at the head of a coalition government. Britain was in a desperate situation as France had fallen but to Churchill it was a situation for which he felt that his earlier life had been but a preparation.

During the five years of his war-time leadership, he devised the destroyers-for-bases deal, lend-lease and the Atlantic Charter, until America came into the war in December 1941.

In opposition after 1945, he campaigned, equally vehemently, for vigilance against a Russia then in occupation of much of Central

63

CHARLES DICKENS

Europe - 'an iron curtain' was
Churchill's phrase. In 1951 he
became Prime Minister at the age
of seventy-seven. On his
resignation in 1955, he became a
back-bencher, to be held in great
veneration on all sides in the House
of Commons. His funeral in 1965
was an occasion of national leave-
taking; the service in St Paul's was
followed by burial in the family
vault at Bladon, near Blenheim,
after journey by barge up the
Thames.

There were many Churchills in
one: the dashing and courageous
young subaltern at Omdurman who
rode in the last cavalry charge in
British history; a great romantic in
the epic age of the Empire, but also
a social reformer as a Liberal in
politics, with fifty-five years as an
MP, thirty of these as a minister;
the statesman with a prophetic view
of Nazi Germany in the early 1930s
and of Stalin's Russia in the late
1940s; the war-leader, living on a
diet of brandy, cigars and crises,

64

inspiring by his zest, convictions,
strategic range and oratory. He
was a popular Caesar, at once
dictator and democrat.

In 1947, Lady Moran, his doctor's
wife, asked him 'Which year of all
your life, if you could relive one
twelve months, would you choose?'
Winston replied, '1940, every time,
every time.'

Dickens, Charles

1812-1870 A poor and sickly child,
his father imprisoned for debt, he
was employed labelling bottles at a
shoe-blacking factory near
Hungerford Bridge. Dickens went
to school in Camden Town but
spent what time he could reading
voraciously in the British Museum.
His first real job was as a solicitor's
clerk in a law firm in Gray's Inn
(he would draw lavishly on law
offices and lawyers for material, as
in *Bleak House* and *The Pickwick
Papers*) and then from 1834 as a
journalist. He was married and the
father of ten children but, as
success came, the marriage
collapsed and he had separated
from his wife by 1858. Articles and
books came in a steady stream.

Despite long spells abroad enjoying
fame (USA where he did readings,
and Italy) he produced almost a
novel a year. By the time of his
death at the age of fifty-eight he
had written fifteen major novels,
many short stories, given readings,
staged private theatricals, made
many speeches and edited a
popular weekly magazine in which
Great Expectations first appeared.
Almost all his writing is London-
based. He walked its streets with
fantastic energy using his
meticulous observation and vivid
imagination. He lived for three
years at 48 Doughty Street, while
working on *The Pickwick Papers*,
Oliver Twist, and *Nicholas Nickleby*.
A Dickens' study-centre and
museum is maintained here with
many of his letters and some of his
furniture. As a newly-wed, Dickens
lived in Furnival's Inn, now
replaced by the redbrick fortress of
the Prudential Assurance Company,
where he began *The Pickwick
Papers*, probably his best-loved
book. Gone also is his home for
nine years on Tavistock Square,
now the massive block designed by
Lutyens for the BMA. Here he
wrote *Bleak House*, perhaps of all
his books the one that best conveys
his sense of the labyrinthine, fog-
bound character of the London of
his day.

Dickens was crusader as well as
story-teller: he was against children
being exploited - as he felt he had
been - against sweated labour, the
brutal poor laws, the horrors of
prison. Newgate, where public
hangings continued until 1868,
fascinated him - as shown in
Barnaby Rudge, in *Great
Expectations* when young Mr Pip
goes to see the yard where the
gallows are kept, and in *Oliver
Twist*, where Fagin awaits his end.

Fleet Street

One of the most ancient
thoroughfares in London; since the
coming of print the street has been
identified with the production of
newspapers. For long, its pubs (Ye
Olde Cheshire Cheese, Ye Olde
Cock Tavern, The Old Bell or El
Vino's wine bar) were the haunts of

journalists from most daily and Sunday newspapers. In recent years with new-style, particularly photo-offset, facilities requiring electricians more than compositors, national newspapers have moved to form part of a new City of London in Docklands.

A host of small printing presses came into existence in the 16th and 17th centuries around nearby Aldersgate. The King James' Version of the Bible was first produced in 1589 by a group of churchmen headed by Lancelot Andrewes, rector of St Giles' in Cripplegate, using a number of small presses in Little Britain and near St Paul's. Milton lived in

Aldersgate and dictated *Paradise Lost* to his printer friends here in 1663. It was from these presses that, in 1719, came the first volume of *Robinson Crusoe*.

Half-way down Fleet Street is the octagonal church of St Dunstan in the West. The 1586 statue of Queen Elizabeth I above the entrance to the vestry porch is the earliest public statue of an English monarch. On the west wall of the nave is the well-known epitaph to Hobson Judkin, which is regarded as unique: 'The Honest Solicitor'. William Tyndale, the later

translator of The New Testament, was preacher here, as was John Donne. Outside the front entrance of the church is the wall slab to Isaac Walton, the fisherman whose *Compleat Angler* was published in 1653; he was a church-warden for many years. Lord Baltimore whose name is carried today by the American city and Atlantic port is buried here. The north-west chapel is used by the Roumanian Orthodox Church. In 1666 the Great Fire halted within yards of St Dunstan's.

Franklin, Benjamin
1706-1790 The American statesman and scientist first came to London in 1725 to work in the Lady Chapel of St Bartholomew the Great, then described as a printer's office. He returned to London for five years from 1757 and again for eleven years from 1764. During these fifteen years, he stayed at 36 Craven Street, off the Strand, the only house in which he lived that is still standing. It is now the Benjamin Franklin House, a small museum, library and educational centre for Anglo-American studies. While working as colonial agent and inventor, Franklin was a convivial spirit in coffee houses, mixing with journalists and authors - his favourite tipple was rum and Madeira. These are now clubs and pubs such as King Lud on Ludgate Hill (the cellars of which once formed part of Newgate Prison); Ye Olde Cheshire Cheese, just off Fleet Street (also the haunt of Dr Johnson, who lived nearby in Gough Square, but who did not like Americans); and The Jamaica off Gracechurch Street, the haunt of sugar-men from the West Indies and Quakers like David Barclay, the founder of Barclays Bank. Franklin returned home on the Pennsylvania Packet in Spring 1775; and the Declaration of Independence, which he helped draft, came a year later.

Great Fire of London
(1666) The fire in all its horror, six months after the plague, at least destroyed much of the shoddy disease-infested houses. The

65

flames, which began when a baker allowed his fires to grow too hot, reached but did not destroy Samuel Pepys' own house. He had already moved all his belongings, and buried his wine and his Parmesan cheese in the garden. Pepys watched the progress of the fire from the tower of the church nearby, All Hallows by the Tower. St Paul's and eighty other churches, the Guildhall, forty-four livery halls, the Royal Exchange and thirteen thousand houses were destroyed.

The fire did more damage than the blitz of world war two and left the area east of Temple Bar a charred wilderness. To replace it, John Evelyn wanted an Italianate city of wide streets and piazzas, Sir Christopher Wren wanted to turn the Fleet River, running along where Farringdon Road now is, into a canal and to ban all noisy trades from the City. Their plans came to naught but the Guildhall was rebuilt in three years, the livery halls followed and, in 1670, fourteen new churches were begun. At least Wren was allowed to design and work on many of the new churches, including St Paul's, and to build the Monument in commemoration.

Greenwich

Henry VIII and Mary and Elizabeth Tudor were born in Greenwich. The palace and the river were always very special to them. Indeed, in Tudor times, the Thames was the royal and the capital's main street and the Thames watermen were the taximen of the 16th and 17th century. Just up-river from Greenwich at Rotherhithe, Christopher Jones, the master of the *Mayflower* is buried in St Mary's parish churchyard. It was from here that the *Mayflower* sailed. Nearby is Deptford, from which in 1732 James Oglethorpe and his settlers sailed to Georgia.

Henry VIII

1491-1547 On the death in 1503 of his elder brother Arthur, who had married Catherine of Aragon for her dowry from Spain, Henry VIII,

the new ruler, contracted to marry her for the same reason. A Renaissance figure, tall, handsome and athletic when young, Henry VIII was a poet and musician, a student of theology and vigorous Defender of the Faith, a title conferred on him by Pope Leo X for his treatise against Luther in 1521. The reasons for his struggle to obtain a divorce were dynastic - a male heir to the throne was essential; sexual - Henry VIII at least married his mistresses; political - reflecting the anti-papal and nationalist spirit that marked the Reformation; and theological - was marriage to a brother's widow valid, and, if not, did this explain the queen's barrenness?

The split with Rome was more an assertion of sovereignty than a denial of Catholicism - the King, like his two daughters, Mary and Elizabeth, had little sympathy with Reformers. He was, however, greedy for the wealth and endowments of the church and irritated by its claims to be an *imperium in imperio*. Most of its wealth in land went to endow colleges notably Christ Church, Oxford, and Trinity College, Cambridge, and into the grasping hands of his subjects - many of the great landed aristocrats of England began by acquiring church lands.

House of Commons

The centre of activity is the Chamber of the House itself, where someone - from 14.30 to midnight or thereabouts - is always on his or her feet. One relic of the centuries when the House used St Stephen's Chapel for its meetings (from 1547 to the fire in 1834) is that members bow to the Speaker's chair on entering and leaving: from the practice of genuflexion to the chapel altar.

The House, as Members of Parliament call it, has the atmosphere of a club. Although in debates in the lower House, MPs are required to address colleagues by the name of the constituency they represent, they come to know each other well - and often make

66

friends across the party divide. They all attend only on important occasions - like Budget Days. When absent, they can always claim to be busy in committee, or in their constituencies - or at Ascot. Conscientious MPs find the hours exhausting: committee meetings almost every morning, formal debates in the Chamber from 14.30

major newspapers or TV channels, who are keen to unearth secrets. If there is an obvious source of leaks of information, it is here. By repute, the most congenial of the bars is - appropriately - that in the House of Lords.

House of Lords
The work of the non-elected House

Windows of Houses of Parliament.

until the day's business is complete or until the Government, which controls the timetable 'gets its business'.
And, at the end of each day, there are adjournment debates, which permit, on the motion to adjourn, any member to air a special grievance or issue affecting his constituents. In practice, members of the House rarely go home before midnight.
Nevertheless there are dining rooms, tea rooms and ten bars.
In one, giving access to the Terrace on the river, MPs may entertain guests (Strangers).
In another (Annie's Bar) they may entertain or be entertained by members of the Press Lobby, accredited representatives of the

of Lords is complementary to that of the elected House of Commons. It is also the highest court of appeal in England; for this purpose only the law lords sit - the Lord Chancellor and any peers who have held high judicial office.
Prominent on the right of the Lord Chancellor, who acts as Speaker in the Lords, sit the lords spiritual: two archbishops, three senior bishops (Durham, Winchester and London) and twenty-one other bishops, according to length of service. They do not confine their comments to matters ecclesiastical. There are 800 hereditary peers, in the descending grades of Duke (26), Marquess (36), Earl (192), Viscount (126) and Baron (482), plus five Countesses and thirteen

Baronesses. Alongside the
hereditary peers are those created
since the passing of the Life
Peerages Act of 1958 - usually
retired members of the Commons.

Johnson, Dr Samuel

1709-1784 Neither Dr Johnson nor
James Boswell, who became his
biographer, were Cockneys - born
within the sound of Bow Bells. But
with London, Johnson is identified:
'He who is tired of London' he said,
'is tired of life.' A poor boy from
Lichfield, unable to stay on at
Pembroke College, Oxford, to
complete a degree course, he came
to London to live by words. For
years he was homeless and
survived by being a hack-writer,
mainly for Edward Cave's
Gentleman's Magazine. He wrote
Rasselas to raise the money for his
mother's funeral.
But from 1747, in eight years of
dedication, his labour of love was
his *Dictionary*, listing, describing
and finding new shades of meaning
for some 40,000 words and
illustrating them with over 100,000
quotations. It is the only dictionary
in the world that can be read from
cover to cover purely for pleasure.
However, Johnson owed his
standing less to his *Dictionary* than
to his meeting with, and friendship
of, James Boswell, who preserved
the record of innumerable
conversations with 'the Great
Cham', treasuring his remarks,
obiter dicta and blunt opinions. On
Scots, of whom - despite Boswell's
Lowland Scots' origins - Johnson
thought little: 'The finest prospect
for a Scot is the high road to
England.' On Americans, then
colonists, Johnson thought of them
as 'escaped convicts or slave-
drivers - good for nothing except a
hanging'.

Jones, Inigo

1573-1652 One of the greatest of
London's architects, Inigo Jones,
was the son of a Smithfield cloth-
worker. He paid two visits to Italy
first as a landscape-painter and
then as a student of Roman
architecture, becoming a particular
admirer of Palladio. While serving

as Surveyor of the King's Works,
the country's major architect, he
built the first truly Classical
building in England, the Queen's
House at Greenwich (begun in 1616
completed in the 1630s); the
Banqueting House in Whitehall
(1619-22); and the nave, transepts
and portico of the old St Paul's. He
laid out Covent Garden (from 1631)
and Lincoln's Inn Fields - this
pattern became a characteristic of
his plans for London and a model
for his successors: a central park or
area, with a square of houses
ranged round it.
Jones, like his successor Wren, had
no formal training in architecture
but his impact on the appearance of
urban London and urban England
is beyond calculation.

Pepys, Samuel

1633-1703 Samuel Pepys was a civil
servant working for the Admiralty
when he began to keep his diary.
He was competent and industrious,
his job brought a house with it and
by the ethical standards of the day
allowed him, as one who ordered
the building and supplying of ships,
to make a fortune on the side. It is
the story of this other side that he
records in the secret diary that he
kept for nine years from 1660.
Pepys became Secretary of the
Navy in 1672 but had to resign in
1679 when unfounded charges of
spying for France imprisoned him
for a time in the Tower. He was
reappointed in 1684.
His eyewitness accounts of the
Coronation, the Plague and the
Great Fire as well as the revealing
pen-portraits of his contemporaries
provide a vivid description of life in
Charles II's London.
He lived near the Tower in
Seething Lane and worshipped in
the nearby church of St Olave
where he and his wife are buried.
In later years he lived in
Buckingham Street, within easy
reach of Charing Cross. He
recorded, 'Went out to the Cross to
see Major-General Harrison
hanged, drawn and quartered;
which was done there, he looking
as cheerful as any man could in the
condition.' In 1669, failing eyesight

No.28 Queen Annes Gate

compelled him to discontinue his journal which he kept in code, and it was not deciphered until 1825.

Plague
The onset of the Great Plague of 1665 was characterized by a fever, and the appearance of black soft swellings on the body, the 'plague tokens'. This has left its legacy in a nursery rhyme:

Ring a-ring o'roses
A pocket full of posies
A-tishoo! A-tishoo!
We all fall down.

The roses signify the rose-coloured rashes and the ring the 'tokens' which indicated plague. The posies were the herbs carried to sweeten the air and the sneezing the symptom of those close to death. All who could left London. Government departments moved out - Pepys sent his wife to Woolwich - schools closed and orders were given by the Lord Mayor to shoot cats, dogs and rats on sight. Pepys calculated that forty thousand dogs and five times

as many cats were destroyed. Seventy thousand Londoners died and churchyards were so full that great pits lined with quicklime had to be dug outside the walls. The air stank with the smell of death; and when plague was diagnosed in a house, everyone was locked in. Grass grew on the streets and few boats moved on the river. All the towns outside London posted watches to prevent Londoners seeking refuge. Ten thousand Londoners took to boats moored on the river - and many of them survived. Not until 1 February 1666 did the king return, and church bells rang. It had had precursors: thirty thousand died in the plague of 1603; forty thousand in that of 1625; but it has not recurred since 1666 - as the brown rat replaced the black.

Queen Anne's Gate
Westminster is rich with quiet, elegant streets tucked off main roads (Barton Street off Great Peter Street, Maunsell Street off

Horseferry Road) not least Queen Anne's Gate off Birdcage Walk. Its houses are almost three centuries old and have a number of blue plaques, evidence of history: Lord Palmerston, who was born at No 20, William Paterson, founder of the Bank of England, lived at No 19 and the lawyer-philosopher-politician Lord Haldane at No 28. A statue of Queen Anne, in whose reign the close was built, stands outside No 11. The National Trust has its offices at No 36 and the British Secret Service, MI5, reputedly has its headquarters along here.

Royal Hospital, Chelsea

For more than 300 years the Chelsea Pensioners, in their scarlet (or winter blue) frock-coats have been a familiar sight in this part of London. Some 500 war veterans, usually former NCOs, live in the Royal Hospital as testament to the generosity of Charles II who founded it in 1682 and whom they salute each Oak Apple Day, 29 May. Christopher Wren designed the buildings - particularly the Figure Court and the Chapel - with later additions from Robert Adam and Sir John Soane.

St Bartholomew the Great

The chancel and transepts of the priory church of St Bartholomew the Great are rare examples of Norman architecture. It was founded by Rahere as an Augustinian Priory in 1123. The early 16th century Prior Bolton's window, a delicately pretty little oriel, on the south side of the clerestory, bears a pun on his name - a bolt and a barrel or tun. After the dissolution of the monasteries much of the church was pulled down or put to other use: the North Transept was used as a blacksmith's forge; the Lady Chapel, built in 1330 and much restored, was a printing office and is where the young Benjamin Franklin worked on his first visit to London. The church reverted to its original use during the 19th century and was restored by Sir Aston Webb in 1897. The font is

medieval. There is a monument to Sir Walter Mildmay, the founder of Emmanuel College, Cambridge, from which many Puritan leaders in 17th century Massachusetts came but Rahere's own tomb, under a 15th century canopy, is dominant. He was as concerned with the bodies as with the souls of the poor and founded also St Bartholomew's hospital to the west of the church, the oldest still-functioning hospital in London.

St Bride

At the foot of Fleet Street is the Church of St Bride with its five-tier, wedding-cake steeple - 'a madrigal in stone'. The tallest of Wren's steeples, it was built after the Great Fire, to a height of seventy-two metres, but lost two metres when it was struck by lightning in 1764. The form of lightning conductor to be fitted was the subject of national controversy and Benjamin Franklin was consulted by George III. Known as the parish church of the Press, it was here that Alsace printer Wynkyn de Worde set up Caxton's presses in the churchyard and produced books for the clergy and notables living close by. Its connections with the Press continued; the cost of restoration, after the building was gutted in world war two, was largely paid for by the Press Association. The reredos is a memorial to Edward Winslow, one of the Pilgrim Fathers, a parishioner and boy apprentice in Fleet Street. Near the font there is a charming bust of Virginia Dare - the first English child born in colonial America; her parents were married in St Bride's.

St Clement Danes

Tradition has it that the church was built by Danish settlers in the 9th century; St Clement the martyr was the patron saint of mariners. After the Great Fire, it was rebuilt by Sir Christopher Wren in the 1680s and beautifully restored once more after it had been virtually destroyed during world war two. The memorial church of the Royal Air Force, it has 900 unit and squadron

St Clement Danes.

badges let into the flooring and many of its fixtures and furnishings have been donated by overseas air forces.

The thirty-five metre tower houses the bells that are supposedly referred to in the famous nursery rhyme with the lines 'Oranges and lemons say the bells of St Clement's'. In the centuries when most goods moved by river, fruit merchants on their way from the Thames to Clare Market and Covent Garden paid a tithe on passing the church. However, it is more likely that the St Clement's referred to in the rhyme is St Clement Eastcheap, by the wharves, where the citrus fruit from the Mediterranean was unloaded.

St James's
Between Jermyn Street and Piccadilly, this Wren church was built in 1682-4 for the Earl of St Albans. Restored after world war two damage, its handsome interior is galleried beneath a barrel-vaulted roof supported by Corinthian pillars. The limewood altarpiece, reredos, font and organ-case are the work of master-woodcarver Grinling Gibbons. Henry Purcell and John Blow supervised the installation of the organ which was a gift from Queen Mary in 1691.

St Martin-in-the-Fields
This 18th century church is perhaps the finest work of James Gibbs with its combination of Classical portico and tower, since widely copied. In 1914 the vicar began the tradition of social service and the Dick Sheppard Chapel commemorates his work. Each evening part of the vaulted crypt, refurbished in 1987, is opened as a shelter for the homeless. Lunchtime concerts are held in the church, appropriately as this was the starting point for the now world-famous Academy of St-Martin-in-the-Fields orchestra and chorus.

St Mary-le-Bow
The famous Bow Bells in this delightful Wren church originally rang as a curfew and it was their distinctive peal which is said to have recalled Dick Whittington from Highgate Hill. Those born within their sound are said to be true Cockneys. The hanging rood over the altar steps is a gift from German churches as an act of reparation after world war two. Outside is a memorial to Captain John Smith, founder of Jamestown, Virginia.

St Mary at Lambeth
Captain William Bligh of the *Bounty* is buried here; he had served with

71

Cook on his third voyage. The church is now the Tradescant Museum of Garden History. The Tradescants, father and son, were famous 17th century botanists. They travelled widely and introduced many new species to Britain; the churchyard is laid out as a garden with plants known at that time. The garden of the house in which they lived, near the church, incorporated many specimens from abroad, now in the Ashmolean Museum, Oxford.

St Olave

After escaping the Great Fire, this 15th century church was badly bomb damaged in 1941. It was restored ten years later. The church has strong ties with Norway and is dedicated to King Olaf (or Olave) and Norway's patron saint. From Seething Lane, access to the church is through an unusual gateway, dated 1658, decorated with skulls. This is from a grim design in a Dutch pattern book of 1633 - an eerie harbinger of the plague that was to come. Pepys and his wife Elizabeth are buried here.

St Paul's Cathedral

Sir Christopher Wren's masterpiece was built of Portland stone after the Great Fire. The dome, thirty-four metres in diameter and the world's second largest, contains the Whispering Gallery. The first cathedral built in England after the Reformation, it is rich in Grinling Gibbon's carvings and ironwork by Jean Tijou. It is also well-peopled with monuments, several hundred have appeared in the body of the church since 1790. St Paul's has numerous chapels, one of which, Jesus Chapel, contains a Roll of Honour of the 28,000 American dead of the second world war. The stained glass windows in this chapel show the insignia of the American states and armed forces in a design depicting the service, sacrifice and resurrection of the fighting man. In the crypt are the resting places of painters, poets, musicians and scientists as well as Britain's greatest soldiers and

sailors. Here also is Sir Christopher Wren's grave, with a plain black slab. On the wall above is the famous phrase composed by his son: *Lector, si monumentum requiris, circumspice* - Reader, if you seek his monument, look around you.

Sherlock Holmes

Sherlock Holmes, the subtle, hawk-eyed amateur detective, was the creation not of a born Londoner but of an Edinburgh-trained doctor who practised at Southsea, Sir Arthur Conan Doyle (1859-1930). His medical training emphasized the importance of scientific deduction, careful observation and meticulous medical diagnosis and his tutor Dr Joseph Bell was the model for Holmes. *A Study in Scarlet* (1887) was the first of a long line of stories in which Sherlock Holmes brilliantly solved a wide variety of crimes.

They were published chiefly in the *Strand Magazine* and collected in *The Adventures of Sherlock Holmes* (1891) and *The Memoirs of Sherlock Holmes* (1894). No 221b Baker Street is now the Headquarters of the Abbey National Building Society and only a forwarding address for enquiries, though callers receive a booklet.

Southwark

Just across the river from London, Southwark was the night-halt for travellers from the west or by the Dover road: here Benjamin Franklin spent his first night on reaching the city in 1757. Distractions were provided: taverns, cock-fighting, bear-baiting and the 'Bishop of Winchester's geese', the ladies of the town. For 500 years Winchester Palace stood here. There was the Clink Jail to cope with criminals. 'In the clink' became and remains a popular phrase for 'in jail'.

John Harvard was born in High Street, Southwark, where his father was the local butcher. He went to America in 1637 and when he died in Boston a year later he left half of his estate - £779 17s 2d - and his library of 320 books to a school 'in

St Pauls

the county of Charleston' then
without a name. The city's General
Court ordered that it 'shall bee
called Harvard College' in memory
of him. There is a memorial chapel
to John Harvard in Southwark
Cathedral, the finest Gothic
building in London after
Westminster Abbey.
For eight years Shakespeare lived
and worked as actor, producer and
playwright at the Globe Theatre in
Southwark. The first performances
of *Hamlet, Julius Caesar, Macbeth*
and eight more of his finest plays
took place in this great theatre
open to the heavens, in front of
3,000 spectators. The too-effective
firing of a cannon during *King
Henry VIII* in 1513 set the theatre

alight; it was rebuilt but swept by
fire again in 1540. Southwark is
now the site for a rebuilt Globe, an
exact replica, a study centre as well
as a theatre. This project owes its
existence largely to the energy and
dedication of Sam Wanamaker, the
Philadelphian-born actor and
producer, who spent twenty years
realising his dream.

Thames, River
As all know who follow the fortunes
of the Boat Race each spring, the
River Thames is a tidal estuary
running 350 kilometres inland.
Where London Bridge stands today
is probably the spot where the
Romans looked for the lowest point
at which they could bridge the

river in AD 43; the first stone
bridge was built on the same site in
1209. On the bridge were houses,
shops, a chapel and gatehouses
which could be closed at night and
on which traitors' heads could be
exposed: as with Jack Cade in 1450
and Sir Thomas More in 1535.
Until Westminster Bridge was built
in 1739, London Bridge was the
only roadway over the river. The
buildings on it were pulled down in
1750. The present structure was
built between 1967 and 1972 - its
predecessor went west, to the USA.
Of today's twenty-six bridges
between Tower Bridge and
Richmond Bridge, London is the
newest, Richmond the oldest, nine
are of cast iron and carry railways
and Tower Bridge, opened in 1894,
is the symbol of the city. At the
beginning of the 18th century,
London's quays handled most of
the country's exports, imports and
re-exports, the latter including
tobacco, sugar, silks and spices.
This traffic grew with colonial trade
and was protected by the
Navigation Acts which limited all
overseas trade to British ships.
Always a busy highway, there were
at least thirty landing places
between Parliament Stairs and
London Bridge where boats waited
to be hired. When the river froze
Frost Fairs were held on the ice.

University of London
The University of London is all too
visible off Russell Square in a great
tower that houses its administrative
staff and library. Grouped around
it are its specialist (mainly
graduate) schools of Oriental and
African Studies, Slavonic Studies
and Tropical Medicine. Within
walking distance are Advanced
Legal Studies, Archaeology and
Classical Studies, Latin American
Studies, Commonwealth Studies,
United States Studies and the
Institutes of Historical Research
and Education. Equally close are
Birkbeck College (strong in social
studies and doing much of its
teaching in the evening);
University College in Gower Street,
first of the under-graduate colleges,
founded in 1826 by a radically-

minded group which included
Jeremy Bentham, who can be seen
sitting (in a preserved state) 'under
the dome' of his college; and King's
College in the Strand, founded by a
rival and more conservative-minded
group, who at first emphasized
theological studies in opposition to
'the godless place' in Gower Street
but one of whose major
departments is now War Studies.

Wellington
1769-1852 Born in Ireland of an
Anglo-Irish family, Arthur
Wellesley, first Duke of Wellington
(1769-1852) is, alongside William
Pitt, first Earl of Chatham, John
Churchill (first Duke of
Marlborough) and Sir Winston
Churchill, one of Britain's four
great war-leaders. Wellington
identified with the struggle against
the French Revolution and
Napoleon, served against the
French Revolutionary armies in
1794 and from 1795 to 1805 in
India, where his elder brother was
Governor-General. He suppressed
the attempt of the Sultan of Mysore
to give assistance to France and
destroyed the Mahratta
Confederacy. These victories laid
the foundation of what became the
British Empire in India, and earned
Wellington the name, not meant as
a compliment by Napoleon, of 'the
Sepoy General'.
When Napoleon, who in 1804 took
the title of Emperor, put his eldest
brother Joseph (later an American
citizen) on the throne of Spain in
1808, Wellington was sent with a
small expeditionary force to
Portugal to attempt to drive the
French back, abetted by
Portuguese and Spanish guerrilla
forces. The Peninsular War
became one of the most successful
military 'side-shows' in history.
With victories at Talavera (1809)
and Salamanca (1812), the French
were defeated in 1814 at Toulouse;
Napoleon abdicated and was
confined on the island of Elba.
Ten months later when Napoleon
escaped and attempted to rally
France once again to his cause,
Wellington with Prussian allies
defeated him at Waterloo (June

Westminster Abbey - north frontage.

1815); Napoleon was then exiled to St Helena, where he died of cancer six years later. As a soldier Wellington was sensible, cautious and totally free from illusions. His troops, he said, were 'the scum of the earth, enlisted for pay'. He showed the same down-to-earth qualities and mordant comment in politics and became Prime Minister in 1828. He believed in the emancipation of Catholics - over which he fought a duel - and persuaded Lords and Commons to accept the repeal of the Corn Laws, which restricted imports of grain, but he opposed the Reform Bill of 1832 and any further extension of the franchise - which brought him bitter unpopularity and led to a mob breaking windows at Apsley

House on the anniversary of Waterloo. The title 'The Iron Duke' referred not to his firmness in command of men, but to the iron shutters he installed in Apsley House.

Westminster Abbey
Consecrated on 28 December, 1065, the Abbey is the finest example of the Early English style though the many tombs, statues and memorials distract from its grandeur. The nave was rebuilt between 1376 and 1388 by Henry de Yevele. Henry V's chantry was added in 1441 and Henry VII's chapel, with its magnificent vaulted roof and banners and crests of the Knights of the Bath, was built in 1509. The west towers are 18th

century additions by Wren and Hawksmoor, his pupil. Buried near the Chapel of St Edward the Confessor are five kings and four queens. At the dissolution of the monasteries in 1540 much of the Abbey's treasure was confiscated and the Benedictine community of some fifty monks disbanded; the monastic school remained. The King's Grammar School, now Westminster School, is still one of the great public schools. The Abbey and its grounds are rich in history: Caxton set up his printing press here in 1476. At the western end of the long high-vaulted nave is a lighted wall case, containing a book of remembrance of the civilian dead of London's blitz; immediately above is a wall plaque commemorating 'a faithful friend of freedom and of Britain', Franklin Delano Roosevelt. Sir Winston Churchill is himself commemorated by a green marble plaque set in the floor of the nave between the west doorway and the grave of the Unknown Soldier.

Westminster Cathedral
Seat of the Cardinal Archbishop of Westminster, this Byzantine-style structure was completed in 1903. Built of red brick with contrasting bands of Portland stone under a roof with four domes, it has the widest nave in England. Its interior vastness and beautiful proportions are impressive. Decorating the main piers are the Stations of the Cross carved in stone by Eric Gill; his work can also be seen in the figures of St John Fisher and St Thomas More in the altarpiece. A square campanile eighty-seven metres high leads off the entrance vestibule.

Whitehall
Whitehall Palace, built in the 13th century was enlarged and enriched by Cardinal Wolsey so extravagantly that Henry VIII annexed it as a palace. It extended from Charing Cross to Westminster Hall and the river. After a fire in 1698, little was done to restore it; the main surviving building is the Banqueting House, built by Inigo

Jones between 1619 and 1622. Included in the palace was the site of a Scottish Royal Palace - James I of England was James VI of Scotland - hence the frequency of references to Scotland along Whitehall: the Scottish Office is at Dover Street; when the London Metropolitan police force was set up in the 1820s, they were given a location in Scotland Yard.
Whitehall is now synonymous with the Civil Service, the faceless men who run the country and whose badges are furled umbrellas, bowler hats and document cases marked by the official symbols, ER. Here are the Treasury, the Foreign and Commonwealth Office and the Ministry of Defence.
In the middle of these great monoliths to bureaucracy is one short street, now prohibited to tourists: Downing Street where, since 1735, Number 10 has been the official residence of the Prime Minister. Built by Sir George Downing in the 1680s, Number 10 was extended and re-furbished between 1960 and 1964.

Wren, Sir Christopher
(1632-1723) A mathematician and physicist, Sir Christopher Wren became Professor of Astronomy at Oxford before turning to architecture - a private interest he had studied in France and Holland. He was engaged on a survey of old St Paul's, planning its repair, when the Great Fire of London gave him his opportunity.
In 1667 he appointed surveyor of the rebuilding and, two years later, Surveyor of the King's Works. Not only did he plan and carry through the new building but he designed wide streets, magnificent quays and more than fifty-one of the churches that replaced those destroyed. Wren was certainly England's greatest church architect and a major secular builder establishing the Classical style: in London he designed the Monument, Marlborough House in Pall Mall, the austere Royal Hospital, Chelsea, and the baroque Greenwich Hospital. ❏

Map reading

From street to square, mews to mall · this index matches each one to the large-scale pull-out map

Each name is listed in alphabetical order. A letter (or letters) and a number (or numbers) after the name are a key to its position on the map. The map is divided into sections, each marked with a letter and a number.